THE
MARINE AQUARIUM HANDBOOK
Beginner to Breeder

by
Martin A. Moe, Jr.

The Norns Publishing Company
Marathon, Florida

Distributed by
GREEN TURTLE PUBLICATIONS
P.O. Box 17925
Plantation, FL 33318

Library of Congress Cataloging in Publication Data.

Moe, Martin A.
  The Marine Aquarium Handbook

  Bibliography: p.
  Includes index.
  1. Marine aquariums. I. Title.
SF457.1.M63   639.3'42   82-3400
ISBN 0-939960-02-08   AACR2
1st Printing April 1982
2nd Printing October 1982
3rd Printing September 1983
4th Printing March 1984
5th Printing December 1984
6th Printing April 1985

COVER PHOTOS:

FRONT: A spawning pair of clownfish, *Amphiprion ocellaris,* peek out from the safe embrace of their anemone. The male clownfish is never very far from the eggs nested on the rock near the anemone. The eggs are only a day away from hatching, as evidenced by the bright eyes of the embryos reflecting light through their transparent egg capsules.

BACK: The Janitor. A hermit crab, *Pagurus* sp. pauses on his clean up rounds to look into the camera.

Printed by Hallmark Press Inc., Miami, Florida

FOREWARD

So you want to go marine. The lure of those brilliant gems of life from far off tropical seas is beginning to get to you. But a good marine aquarium set up is a bit expensive, and you have heard that the failure rate of new marine aquarists is frighteningly high, and even though fresh water aquaria hold no fears for you, the big step to salt water gives you the trembles. Well, you are not alone and your fears are not without some justification. Most of the failures with marine aquaria are due to lack of knowledge of the biological processes that occur in the aquarium. The marine aquarium is a miniature ecosystem, the interactions of living organisms are what makes it work and the living balance of the aquarium is as delicate as life itself. Although it is these same processes that keep a fresh water aquarium in good health, the "balance" of a marine aquarium has a narrow edge and requires at least a basic understanding of the factors that create a healthy marine aquarium.

Many people have asked me in the last few years how to go about setting up a marine tank, and I have been happy to give them what advice I could in 30 minutes or so of conversation. This is usually inadequate, however, because one often does not remember everything that is said, and one seldom remembers to say everything. The intent of this book is to present in simple, basic language the information necessary to develop a successful marine aquarium and to know why it is successful. And those that wish to try their hand at breeding marine fish will find all they need to know to spawn and rear some of the most popular marine aquarium fish in a home environment. It is not designed to be an expensive picture book or a dry laboratory manual, there are many of these available today that serve specific needs. It is an information book, a hobbyists handbook that is enjoyable to read and provides basic understandings and working techniques as well.

To my parents -

Whose support and encouragement were neverfailing.

CONTENTS

INTRODUCTION

Most of the Earth is ocean — and of the aquatic environments of the world, coral reefs are among the most environmentally stable and biologically dynamic. Coral reefs only occur within about 30 degrees of latitude from the equator. They can only live and grow where average annual water temperatures are 73 to 77 degrees F, salinity is constant and high, and sunlight strongly penetrates the shallow, clear oceanic water. The environment changes little from season to season, year to year; but the animals and plants endlessly combat each other for food and space. These elements of existence have created a wonderland of form, color, and behavior — a wonderland that we can capture, in small measure, in our home aquarium. The romance and mystery of tropic seas can be reflected in a small simulated coral reef snug in one's living room while winter winds pile snow against the door. Not so long ago, 20 years or so, a successful marine aquarist was regarded with awe and wonder as one favored by Neptune himself and thus privy to the secrets of the deep. Now we know that those pioneering individuals were not specially favored but only had the courage to persist, despite failures, and the tenacity to stick with methods that worked for them. However, experience and research accumulate knowledge, and although maintaining a marine aquarium is not as easy as keeping a fresh water tank, most of the questions now have answers and with a little effort the average fish fancier can be a successful marine aquarist.

Three very important, relatively recent developments have put a marine aquarium within reach of most aquarists. These are the development and commercial availability of the all glass tank, wide distribution of synthetic sea salts, and the understanding of the biological functions of the undergravel filter. These basic developments made possible the rapid and extensive growth of the marine segment of the tropical fish hobby. The major innovation yet to flower, but now waiting in the bud, is the commercial propagation of many species of marine tropical fish. When this occurs, the marine aquarium hobby, and control and preservation of the tropical fish resources of coral reefs, will truly come of age. It is now possible for the home aquarist to spawn and rear certain species of marine fish. Certainly it is more difficult to breed marine fish than it is to rear guppies and goldfish, but the knowledgeable and determined home hobbyist can achieve some success in this area, and I write here from actual experience.

A trouble free, entertaining and rewarding display is the goal of most marine aquarists and I hope this book will contribute to that end. I have directed it toward those that need an accurate, easily understood guide to the basics of marine aquarium keeping. The emphasis is on simple techniques that work, low cost methods, and the how and why of what happens in a marine aquarium. It discusses topics as basic as tank set up and as advanced as breeding, thus should be useful to the old hand as well as the beginning marine aquarist.

Chapter 1

THE AQUARIUM
Size, Shape and Construction

The first decision you make after you decide to become a marine aquarist usually concerns the container that will house your own private few cubic feet of ocean bottom. This basic choice of a tank will have a great effect on your future success and on the type and size of fish and invertebrates you can maintain. If this is your first marine aquarium you should ask yourself some basic questions about your plans and intentions before you buy or build a tank. Some good questions are: How much money do I want to spend? Do I want to start with a large tank (because large tanks are more biologically stable) and work with it until I know what I'm doing, or do I want to start with a small tank of 20 gallons or less (because the investment is much less) and then get a large tank when I know what I'm doing? Do I want to keep exotic tropical marine fish or just local critters? Should I build my own tank and filter to save money or should I buy commercially made equipment? How much space, money and time do I have to devote to a marine aquarium? You are the only one who can answer these questions since you are the only one that can provide the information, but it makes sense to get as much knowledge as possible before you make the plunge. Read everything you can find and talk to good dealers and successful aquarists. Don't automatically believe everything you read and hear, because there is a lot of inaccurate information around as well as experimentally verified facts. A good marine hobbyist always thinks, and experiments to find the techniques that work best for them.

Contrary to some existing opinions a marine aquarium can be maintained in a 10 gallon tank, a 5 gallon tank, and even a 1 gallon jar, if one so desired. The same biological systems will work in one gallon as well as 300 gallons, but the smaller the system, the easier it is to overcrowd and there is less "reserve" filtration capacity. I would recommend a 20 gallon tank to a beginner because this is large enough keep an interesting number and variety of fish with adequate filtration capacity, and is still small enough to be manageable and economical. Also, if you do graduate to a larger tank, the 20 gallon makes a good second tank for treatment or quarantine. Another thing to consider on the size of your tank is weight. This may seem obvious, but if you overlook it you could be in a peck of trouble. One gallon of sea water weighs 8½ pounds, which isn't an awful lot, but 50 of them together weigh 425 pounds and 100 gallons weigh 850 pounds. Its a little disquieting to come home after a rough day at work and find your new 100 gallon marine tank in the apartment underneath yours, which, I have heard, has happened before.

The shape of a marine tank is important because it can affect the filtering capacity of the tank, and thus the number of fish that the tank can carry. The more surface area in the filter, which covers the bottom of the tank, the greater the number of fish that the tank can safely support. Therefore, a low flat tank with an undergravel filter has a slightly greater filtering capacity than a high sided tank of the same gallonage. If you really want a high style tank because the fish have greater depth to swim, or because it fits the planned placement of the tank, or because you just like that style better; go ahead and get it. The difference in filtering capacity is not that great. A marine tank can be any shape you wish providing that the filter is large enough to carry the biological load residing in the tank. You can even have an inverted pyramid if you wish, but better plan on a filter outside the tank if this is the case.

Unless you want an exceptionally large tank or a very unusual shape, the only way to go is with an all glass aquarium. Avoid any tanks with metal or exposed concrete or wood. There are many companies that manufacture all glass tanks and one should shop for price and quality as with any other purchase. Because of the fragile nature of a glass box, it is always wise to inspect it carefully before you truck it home. Watch for cracks, of course, but also be aware of more subtle defects. Are the edges of the tank chipped, and if so, do the chips break through or damage the silicone seals? If it is a large tank, is the bottom piece made from glass a size thicker than the sides? Is the reinforcement about the top and bottom well made, totally plastic, and firmly attached? Is the silicone seal evenly distributed along all seams? Check for disruptions of the seal by viewing the edge through the overlapping side. Numerous air bubbles and channels through the seal may indicate potential leaks and glass cuts that are not perfectly square. If the glass is not cut square, cracks and leaks will probably occur, especially in large tanks. Buy your tank from a good dealer, one recommended by other aquarists, and you will get a good tank and good advice.

You may, if you are a handy sort of person, decide that to save money and fulfill a creative urge, you should build your own tank. If you plan to charge for your time and trouble, forget it and buy a tank. However, building your own tank does have some advantages. First you will save money, second, you can build any size or shape you wish to fit any placement you desire, and third, it adds a unique and creative dimension to the hobby. Since I have built all my own tanks, I can give you a few tips on construction. It doesn't pay to build your own tank unless you use ¼ inch *salvage* plate glass. This is glass that has been salvaged from windows and showcases and is generally worn and a little scratched, but still satisfactory for an aquarium. Turn the scratched side inward and when water fills the scratches they will disappear. Give the glass shop the *exact* measurements for each piece of glass you need, specify salvage plate glass, and tell them that all pieces must be cut square and exact to measurements because they are to be part of an aquarium. If you use new ¼ inch plate glass or build a tank as large as 50 gallons or more and need glass thicker than ¼ inch, the cost may equal or exceed a commercially available tank.

Your tank will be glued together with a silicone rubber sealer available in aquarium shops and hardware stores. Dow Corning and General Electric both make a good silicone sealer. Some types of these silicone sealers are manufactured for use on boats and in bathrooms and have a mildewcide incorporated in the sealer. If you make your tank with silicone rubber that has been so treated there will be much weeping and wailing and gnashing of teeth. The safest course is to use only a product that specifies itself as an aquarium sealer on the label. Working with this silicone rubber is quite an experience. I can only describe the un-cured texture as a mixture of library paste and chewing gum scraped up off a hot sidewalk. It sticks to your fingers, to the glass, to your pants, your face and the table; it gets on the glass where you don't want it and never quite gets all over every edge where it must be. It is great fun, however, to peel it off your hands in long, thin strips when you finish. Its good stuff to have around even if you don't build your own tank because it fixes leaks very well and repairs numerous household items. I advise you to practice working with the silicone sealer before starting, especially if your want a neat, professional tank when you finish.

Now, if you still want to build your own tank, here are the dimensions and construction instructions for a 20 gallon tank of convenient shape. I prefer to have the sides rest on top of the bottom piece, although I have seen some aquariums with the sides surrounding the bottom.

Materials

All glass pieces are ¼ inch plate glass with seamed edges. (The edges are seamed with a grinding machine to remove the razor sharp edges. You can do the same thing with fine sandpaper or a file and reduce the cost of the glass.)

Dimensions

3 pieces, 30" × 12½"
(bottom, front and back sides)

2 pieces, 12" × 12½"
(left and right ends)

1 piece, 12" × 3"
(center brace, optional)

One 3 oz tube, silicone rubber sealer

Procedure

Note that the bottom, front, and back sides are all the same dimensions. Pick the best piece for the front side and the worst piece for the bottom. Clean all the pieces with a commercial glass cleaner, wipe them clean and dry and lay them out on a table with the sides surrounding the bottom next to the edge where they will stand. Be sure to put a drop cloth or newspaper under the work area so that the woman (or man) in your life will not verbally abuse you.

This aquarium will be 30" long and 12¾" high. The sides will stand on top of the bottom and the ends will fit inside the front and back sides. It is easier to apply the silicone sealer to the edges of the side to be applied rather than to the bottom and the existing sides. Building the aquarium should be done all at one time so that you get a continuous seal from the sealer. You have five to ten minutes to put the whole thing together, and after its done, leave it alone until the silicone cures. The more you push and wiggle it, the more problems you create. Try to set each piece into place with a minimum of adjustment.

The first piece to set in place is the back side. Run a thin bead of sealer along the bottom edge and carefuly place the side on the back edge of the bottom piece. Now you've got a problem. You can't let go of the back side or it will fall over, but you have to let go to add one of the ends to the tank. The best thing to do is to have someone hold the back side upright in position while you continue with an end, however, it is possible to place a heavy object close to the back side so that it leans against it slightly and does not fall over. This is the most delicate part of the whole operation.

Once the back is securely supported, run a thin bead of sealer along the bottom and back edge of one end and carefuly and gently press it into place. Take care that you don't push the back side off the bottom during this second step. As the end attaches to the back side and bottom piece, the two upright sides will support each other and bracing or holding is no longer necessary. Masking tape is often recommended to help hold the sides to the bottom and to each other, but unless the tank is quite large or the glass is not cut square, I find that it is not worth the bother to use tape or other supports. The other end is the next piece to attach. Once again run a thin bead of sealer along the bottom and back edge of the end piece and carefully and gently press it into place. Take care once again that you do not push the back side off the bottom piece.

Now the only piece left is the front side. Run a thin bead of sealer along the edges of the upright ends and along the bottom edge of the front side. Hold the front side at an angle so that you can first place the bottom of the side on the edge of the aquarium bottom and then carefully push the front piece into place against the upright ends. Some of the sealer will squeeze out from between the glass on the inside and outside of the tank. Don't fiddle with the sealer on the outside until after it cures and then use a razor blade to cut it off cleanly with the outside glass. Don't pull it off because this may cause leaks. The sealer on the inside can also be cut off after curing and this gives the tank a neat professional appearance. However, I prefer to use a small wooden or

Figure 1. The completed 20 gallon tank. This one has been in hatchery use for 10 years and is still very serviceable. Note the patches on the bottom. Chips and cracks can be easily and permanently repaired by cementing a small piece of glass directly over the break with silicone sealer.

metal spreader and carefully train the inside bead into a thin wedge along every inside corner of the tank. This must be done within a few minutes of application, before the sealer forms a surface skin. If this is done carefully the appearance of the tank is not affected and insurance against leakage is obtained.

The brace is the last piece to be added. This tank does not really need a brace, but I usually put one in the center for additional strength, which is needed in a commercial situation. Wait about 24 hours until the tank has cured before attaching the brace. The brace extends from the top center of the front side to the top center of the back side and is designed to fit in-between the sides and flush with the top edge of the tank. The brace could be cut a half inch longer and be placed on the top of the sides, but this placement may cause problems with covers and lights. The tank can be placed on its side to apply the brace so it won't slip down while curing or the brace can be supported from the bottom while it cures. The same general procedure can be used to construct tanks to your own specifications. You can use a little imagination and custom design tanks in many different shapes.

Its even possible to make a tank within a tank and have fresh water fish in one compartment and marine fish in another, or even build a terrarium inside the fish tank.

Breeding marine fish requires a separate tank for the pelagic larval stage of marine fish. The tank described above was used as a juvenile tank to hold and grow small clownfish after they had passed through the larval stage. A good larval tank should have a little higher side design to provide a higher water column for the pelagic (free swimming) larval fish. A 36 gallon tank with the general dimensions of 18″ wide by 26″ long by 18″ high works well to rear up to a couple of hundred anemonefish through the larval stage.

Chapter 2

THE WATER

Composition, Collection and Manufacture

Should one use natural or synthetic sea water in a marine aquarium? This question is almost always sure to spark a lively discussion. Cries of POLLUTION! BACTERIA! and ORGANIC OVERLOAD! arise from one corner and are met by shouts of NATURAL COMPOSITION! COMPLETE TRACE ELEMENTS and ESSENTIAL ORGANIC COMPOUNDS! reverberating from the other. Let's take a look at the composition of natural sea water and this will give us some clues on how to use it in a marine aquarium. Sea water is an extremely complex and dynamic fluid when all of its inorganic and organic constituents are considered. Fortunately you don't have to have a degree in marine chemistry to be able to set up and maintain a marine aquarium, but it is helpful to know what kinds of things make up natural sea water, especially if you plan to use Mother Nature's formula. The components of natural sea water can be put into four broad classifications.

The first of these is pure water, the ultimate solvent. Water represents about 96% of all the stuff in a bucket of sea water. This is the part that evaporates off, causes rain, and leaves everything else behind in the form of a white, crusty residue. Obviously it is the stuff left behind in the bucket that makes sea water so different from fresh water.

The second component of sea water goes under the broad term of inorganic solids and gases. All the dissolved salts, trace elements, inorganic pollutants and dissolved gases belong in this category; which, except for the gases, usually make up over 99% of the crusty white stuff at the bottom of the bucket. Only seven kinds of salts (sodium chloride, magnesium chloride, magnesium sulphate, calcium sulfate, potassium sulfate, calcium carbonate and potassium or sodium bromide) make up over 99½% of all the conservative elements in sea water. The conservative elements are the ones that do not change in proportion to each other regardless of the total amount of dissolved matter. In other words, the percentage of sodium chloride, for example, in the total salt content is always the same whether the sea water is half strength or full strength. This is very important, for this is why

10

sea water varies so little all over the world and is such a stable, life supporting environment. The remaining half percent of the inorganic solids is made up of at least 60 elements found in such tiny amounts that they are called trace elements and a variable amount (depending on where the water is taken) of pollutants, such as mercury, that are released by man's activities. Even though the trace elements are present in extremely tiny amounts, some of them (especially zinc, copper, iodine, vanadium, cobalt, molybdenum and arsenic) are essential to many living organisms. Some animals and plants can accumulate these trace elements in their own bodies in concentrations thousands of times greater than the surrounding waters and some of these elements are even depleted in areas of the sea due to the activity of marine life.

If this can happen in the open sea, it can certainly occur in a marine aquarium where the ratio of life to water is much greater. These elements are not always released back into the water when the micro-organism dies, and if you remove algae from your tank, you are also removing accumulated trace elements. Therefore, it is wise to replenish the trace elements in your tank every month or so if you do not make a water change with natural sea water or a complete salt mix.

The third basic classification of the stuff of sea water is dissolved organic substances. These are compounds such as amino acids, proteins, enzymes, vitamins and pigments. Inshore waters carry a greater loading of dissolved organics than clear offshore waters. Natural toxins are sometimes found in sea water also, especially during reproductive "blooms" of minute marine algaes. These blooms are usually called red tides and can be very destructive to fish life. Some of the dissolved organic substances originate from life in the sea. They are given off by animals, plants and bacteria during the normal process of living and are also liberated in death. Run off water from the land adds greatly to the organic content of nearshore waters, and man contributes ever increasingly to this category through discharge of petroleum products, sewage and agricultural and industrial wastes. These effluents add a number of toxins such as PCB's that can be accumulated in the tissues of marine animals, and also, basic nutrients from sewage that enrich inshore waters and cause heavy growths of planktonic algae.

Life is the fourth category of things to be found in that bucket of sea water. No matter how clear the water, there is an astonishing number and variety of living things to be found.

Bacteria and microscopic plants and animals occur in each drop of inshore water. Some of these, such as larval fish and crabs, have the potential for great growth; while others, such as one celled algae and copepods, remain as tiny planktonic creatures throughout their brief existence. Life is ever accumulating and assimilating the elements of the sea, containing them, using them and liberating them in death and excretion. Thus the sea is a dynamic fluid, filled with life, accepting nutrients from the land and energy from the sun and balancing the existence of life on earth upon the complex interactions of the life within its waters.

I hope the above discussion makes it easier to understand that a marine aquarium is not a tiny slice of a coral reef or ocean bottom, and that a bucket of sea water and a bucket of marine aquarium water are two entirely different things. How do they differ? Water from a marine aquarium has the same four basic categories of constituents; water, dissolved inorganics, dissolved organics and life. Water and the conservative constituents (basic salts) are the same in both buckets, but the other, nonconservative constituents differ greatly. Trace element composition changes rapidly because once captive life forms use them, they are not replenished by the vast volume of the sea. Dissolved organics are not as diffused and reused in a marine aquarium as they are in the sea thus they accumulate from the wastes of animals to a great degree. These wastes are converted to basic nutrients with proper biological filtration, but the concentrations of these nutrients can be hundreds of times greater in the bucket of aquarium water than in the bucket of raw sea water. Living things are also found in both buckets, but all the tiny plants and animals in sea water do not exist in aquarium water. Bacteria are the primary life forms in aquarium water. The numbers of bacteria in one cubic centimeter of sea water varies from less than 10 in offshore waters to several hundred or more in clear inshore waters. In contrast, marine aquarium waters may contain several hundred thousand or more in each cubic centimeter. All bacteria are not bad, however, and their presence in aquarium water does not necessarily make it worse than raw sea water, just different.

COLLECTING SEA WATER

If sea water were composed of only pure water and dissolved salts and trace elements, collection and use in an aquarium would pose few problems. It is the dissolved organics and planktonic life forms that cause problems for the intrepid aquarist. As soon as the sea water is contained and is no longer part and parcel of the world's oceans, most of the planktonic plants and animals die and bacteria proliferate mightily. Eventually all the remains of planktonic creatures are decayed by bacteria, which also utilize some of the dissolved organics.

Most bacteria need a surface of some sort to work on and the sides of the container, precipated organics and dead plankton provide much more surface area than an equal volume of open sea water. These and other factors result in a fantastic proliferation of bacteria in captive sea water, sometimes to levels of several million per cubic centimeter. This is why many authors suggest that newly collected sea water be kept in the dark for two weeks or more before use, for after that period, most of the organic matter has been utilized, oxidized and precipitated and all the dead plankton has been consumed by bacteria. Bacteria levels then drop to 10 to 100,000 per cubic centimeter. A brownish floculant material accumulates at the bottom of the container and one is instructed to remove the clear water without stirring up the sediment on the bottom.

Below, I describe three ways to process collected natural sea water. The first is the classical, sure way and the second is the lazy man's somewhat risky method. The third is an experimental method that I have had good success with, but one that I can not unconditionally recommend because I don't really know *exactly* what it does to the water and I don't know what effect it might have on many species that have not experienced water so treated.

The first thing to do is to decide where the water is to be obtained. Of course the very best water would be clear offshore water that requires a boat for collection, but your aquarium will operate just as well on carefully collected inshore water. Take your water from an area that has good tidal flushing and no obvious nearby sources of pollution. Avoid sewer outlets, industrial plants and fresh water creeks and rivers. Don't collect water from areas that show an oil or chemical slick on the surface. Also, look for live fish, crabs and other life in the area, and if native fish are present and appear healthy, your water should be good. Anyone who lives near the coast should be able to collect good sea water for an aquarium. When you have found the right site and time, you are ready to collect. One thing you don't want is a car full of 50 gallons of salt water. A good, inexpensive way to transport salt water is with the lowly 20 gallon plastic garbage can.

The more plankton and particulate material that can be

removed when the water is collected, the better the water will be for your aquarium. Use two buckets, a big plastic funnel and some fine filtering material. Several folds of clean cloth, a one inch thickness of pure polyurethane foam or several layers of filtering floss packed into the funnel will do a good job. Line the plastic garbage can with a thin polyethylene bag and fill it with filtered water. Leave some room to twist off and secure the bag with a rubber band or wire twist tie and you have a spill proof container to carry home your water.

The best way to treat the water after you get it home is to store it in the dark for two or three weeks prior to using it in the aquarium. Then remove the water carefully so that the sediment on the bottom of the container is not disturbed. The lazy man's way is to use the water immediately and don't bother with storage or treatment. Sometimes you can get away with this approach with no problems at all if the water is well filtered. Frequently, however, small parasites are introduced this way and can cause hair-pulling, breast-beating problems.

The third way of treating your newly collected water is still experimental. However, water treated this way is routinely used to culture marine tropical fish so the method seems acceptable to most marine organisms. You will need some granular dry chlorine, the type used in swimming pools (65% calcium hypochlorite with no additional algacides), or pure chlorine bleach, an OTO test kit for chlorine (available where swimming pool supplies are sold) and chlorine neutralizer. Sodium thiosulfate is the base for most commercial dechlorinators and is also sold in camera shops as hypo, however, if you use hypo be sure to get pure hypo without film hardners. Add a small measure of chlorine to newly collected water until there is at least five parts per million (ppm) chlorine according to your test kit. Let the water sit with light aeration for 12 to 24 hours and test once again for chlorine. If no chlorine is indicated, this means that you have water with a high organic load and you should treat it once again with chlorine. It also means that the dose of chlorine should be doubled if water is collected from the same location again. Chlorine kills all life in the collected water, including bacteria, and oxidizes the organic matter dissolved in natural sea water. After the water has been chlorinated for 12 to 24 hours it will be very clear and smell like a swimming pool. Now add the sodium thiosulfate in small measure until your test kit indicates that no chlorine remains. It is best to dissolve the sodium thiosulphate in

Figure 2. Granulated chlorine for swimming pools and the OTO test kit for free chlorine. Most chlorine test kits also test for pH, however, the pH range in these kits is usually 7.0 to 7.8, a bit below the range of a marine aquarium. The most effective use of the chlorine test is to tell the aquarist when all free chlorine has been eliminated from the water.

water before adding it to the chlorinated sea water. It won't take much so just add a little at a time until you can estimate how much is required.

Now your water is sterile and may have a slight cloudy appearance. This will clear by itself if the water is left to settle for a day or two under light aeration, or it can be filtered through floss and charcoal for a few hours to clear it even faster. In emergencies, I have used water immediately after neutralization with no ill effects, but I don't recommend it as a general practice. To my knowledge, this method of treating natural sea water is quite safe, but I have not used water so treated for many species of invertebrates, which may be more sensitive to loss of trace elements and vital organic molecules than fish. We have collected water heavily contaminated with oil waste, decaying fish, red tide organisms and toxins, silt and organic matter; treated it with this method; and then used it 24 hours later to rear clownfish and neon gobies. Old aquarium water can also be rejuvenated with this treatment, but repeated treatments will lower the pH of the water and the effect of this water treatment on invertebrates, especially repeated use, is unknown to me.

15

SYNTHETIC SEA WATER

If you happen to live in Omaha, Nebraska, you may have a tough time deciding whether to go to the Pacific, Atlantic or Gulf of Mexico to get your salt water. Even if you live only a few miles from a salt water source, however, you may not want the hassle of cans, buckets, filters and hauling water in the back seat of your Mercedes. Fortunately there is a solution for your problem. You can buy a package of synthetic sea salts from your aquarium dealer and carry home the equivalent of 50 or 100 gallons of salt water in a neat little package on the seat of your car. Synthetic sea water may not be the same thing as natural sea water, but the major brands available today will support marine life in your aquarium almost as well as the real thing, and perhaps even better in some circumstances.

Synthetic sea water differs from nature's own in that the concentrations of the major inorganic salts are not exactly the same, inorganic trace elements are not the same in number or concentration, there are no dissolved organics and, *a very important consideration*, all impurities present in the make up water become part of the aquarium's watery environment. This last point is one that could easily be an overlooked problem. One could figure, "Well, I've got this fine grade of expensive sea salt mix manufactured under exacting conditions from carefully tested, time proven formulas. I mix it with the water I drink, so what could possibly be wrong." I hope that at least 99% of the time this is a totally correct attitude, however, remember that the fresh water supply in some areas of the country may be plagued with bacterial contamination (probably not a problem in a marine tank), industrial waste contamination, concentrations of heavy metals (copper, zinc), extreme hardness and detergent contamination. If there is a suspicion about the purity of your water supply, if you drink and cook with bottled water rather than tap water, then it's a good idea to filter the fresh water through activated carbon before making up the salt water mix. This will take out most of the impurities and get you closer to the final solution that the manufacturer of the salt mix intended.

Follow the manufacturer's instructions when you mix the salts and add the trace elements, after all they ought to know the best way to handle their own product. If you are just setting up a new tank, you can mix the first batch right in the tank, but if you are changing water in an established tank, it is best to mix the salts in a plastic garbage can. Wait until the solution clears and all

16

the elements are dissolved before adding the newly mixed water to your tank. Some of the elements may not dissolve, even after 24 hours of aeration and will form a white precipate on the container bottom. Don't worry about this residue unless it is remarkably excessive, just go ahead and use the water and if some of the sediment gets into the tank its nothing to be concerned about. The low chlorine content of tap water usually disappears when the salt mix is added and is of no concern since the mix is aerated for several hours before use. If there is a question of residual chlorine, a few drops of sodium thiosulphate or a commercial dechlorinator will set your mind at ease.

Unfortunately, in many areas of the country it is no longer possible to dismiss chlorine in tap water with a few drops of a dechlorinator. Due to recent implementation of Environmental Protection Agency regulations on organics in water supplies, municipal water companies are changing the way they treat our tap water. Ammonia is being added to eliminate trihalomethane, a suspected cancer-causing agent. In the past, tap water received only a charge of free chlorine to keep it pure and free of bacteria until it reached our kitchens and bathrooms. Free chlorine is volatile and soon disappears from standing or aerated water and can be quickly eliminated with a little sodium thiosulphate.

When ammonia and chlorine are both present in fresh water, however, they form a stable chloramine compound that is toxic to fish just as free chlorine and ammonia are toxic. Chloramine, unfortunately, does not readily escape from standing water and can not be removed by a standard application of sodium thiosulphate. When ammonia is already present in the water and the amount of chlorine added is below the "break point reaction" level, then chloramine is formed. If enough chlorine is added to exceed the break point reaction level, the chlorine becomes free chlorine and the ammonia is no longer bonded. Both chlorine and ammonia can then escape as gases over a period of time. As long as chlorine levels are maintained under the break point reaction level, chlorine and ammonia are present as the stable chloramine compound. When sufficient ammonia is present in ground water supplies, chloramine is formed when the treatment plant adds only enough chlorine to stay below the break point reaction. If ammonia levels are not sufficient in the raw water supply, it is added by exposing the water to pellets of ammonium sulphate or adding liquid anhydrous ammonia before it is chlorinated. Hatcheries, shops and hobbyists in Texas and Florida have reported considerable loss of livestock due to this development in water treatment technology. If the chloramine levels in your water supply exceed 2 ppm it may be necessary to remove it from the water before setting up an aquarium.

There are ways that the hobbyist can clear fresh water of chloramine *before* making up a synthetic sea water mix. One of the two basic methods described below should work depending on the particular problems presented by the local water supply. The first and easiest method is to add double the dose of sodium thiosulphate (or a commercial dechlorinator) than would ordinarily be necessary to dechlorinate the water. This should break the chloramine bond and chemically remove the chlorine after a working time of two to three hours. Aeration of the water will allow the ammonia to escape as a gas over a period of several hours (longer if the concentration of ammonia is high). The water can be filtered through an ammonia absorbent material, the clay clinoptiolite (zeolite) or a similar commercial product for more positive ammonia removal. It is more important to remove ammonia when preparing water for a partial water change in an established tank than setting up a new tank since the run in period for a new tank will eliminate any ammonia in the water.

The second method is more involved but may be necessary under some local conditions. First, enough chlorine must be added to break the stable chloramine bond and put all chlorine present into the free state. Addition of 1 cc of laundry bleach (no additives) to one gallon of water (one teaspoon Clorox, 5.25% sodium hypochlorite, per five gallons) usually accomplishes this after one hour of aeration. Once all the chlorine is in a free state, it can be removed by traditional methods. Addition of sodium thiosulphate until no chlorine registers on an OTO swimming pool test kit is the standard method of chlorine removal. Mix about 4 oz of sodium thiosulphate to one quart of water to make the treatment solution. Start with 5 drops for each 10 gallons of water to be dechlorinated. Retreat if the OTO test shows that chlorine is still present 5 to 10 minutes after the initial treatment.

Activated carbon filtration after chlorine removal is also a good idea, for although it won't remove ammonia, it will take out any residual chlorine. A final filtration of the fresh water through an ammonia absorbent material will remove the ammonia if this is desired. Don't just soak a bag of ammonia absorbent or activated carbon in the water as this is most inefficient. Set up a filter arrangement to recirculate the water through the filter material.

Which brand of synthetic sea salts should you use? I've tried several and they all seem to do a good job. You should rely on your dealers recommendation or the recommendation of experienced fellow hobbyists in your area. Unless your area has special fresh water problems, any of the major brands of synthetic sea salts mixed with clean, fresh water will provide a good life supporting medium for marine animals and should be the most stable and trouble free element in the whole system.

Synthetic sea salts are easy to keep and store. One can keep it in the package in a dry, cool place ready for mixing and use whenever necessary, or if immediate emergency use is anticipated, it can be dissolved and stored in dark containers ready for instant use. Be sure to label the container carefully if you do this so you will know the date, brand, concentration and any other pertinent information about the mix that should be known when it is used.

Synthetic sea salts have been widely available under numerous brand names for only about the last 15 years. However, the concept and practice of mixing various salts to support marine life in an artificial environment is far older than this. Many formulas have been published during the last 50 years for scientists and advanced aquarists to use in formulating their own experimental synthetic sea salt mixes. In fact, in 1884, H.E. Hoffman published a formula for artificial sea water in Vol. 9 of the Bulletin of the U.S. Fish Commission. It consisted of 13¼ gallons of well water, 46½ oz. of sodium cloride, 3½ oz. of magnesium sulphate, 5¼ oz. magnesium chloride, and 2 oz. of potassium sulphate. Each salt is dissolved separately and then all solutions are mixed and allowed to rest before use. This formula, simple compared with todays claims of 70 trace elements, supported marine life but produced, at best, inconsistent results. If you really want to mix up your own synthetic sea salts, you might try the formula published by Lyman and Fleming in 1940 in an article titled, "The Composition of Sea Water" which appeared in the Journal of Marine Research, No. 3, Vol. 134.

Sodium cloride	23.477 grams	Potassium bromide	0.096 grams
Magnesium chloride	4.981 ''	Boric acid	0.026 ''
Sodium sulphate	3.917 ''	Strontium chloride	0.024 ''
Calcium chloride	1.102 ''	Sodium fluoride	0.003 ''
Potassium chloride	0.664 ''	Water to a total of	1000 grams
Sodium bicarbonate	0.192 ''		

The above formula makes up only 1000 grams or one liter (0.9 quarts) of solution. Multiplying each ingredient by 100 will make up close to 25 gallons of solution and be much easier to weigh out the chemicals. Adding some natural sea water or commercially available trace elements should round out the solution and make a good grade of synthetic sea water. Mixing your own really isn't worth it today because of the availability of commercial brands, but its good to know that you could do it, if you had to.

Good water quality is very important in rearing marine tropical fish, but it may not be as critical as one would suppose. The larval fish has membranes that protect its internal environment from the great concentrations of bacteria and inorganic and organic molecules that surround it and this barrier is effective from the moment of hatch. So although water quality must be good, it need not be a sterile laboratory medium or even duplicate the clear offshore waters that are the natural environment of most larval fish.

The water quality of a balanced, well maintained marine aquarium is quite adequate for survival of most larval marine fish if all other factors such as food, light, temperature and freedom from predators are also adequate. Marine fish have been easily reared in several types of synthetic sea water mixes as well as a variety of natural sea waters. The rearing tank can be set up with natural sea water processed as usual for a marine aquarium, synthetic sea water aged a few days, or even water taken from a disease free, uncrowded aquarium. In fact, water from a marine aquarium carries an initial load of the "good" bacteria that will aid the chemical balance of the rearing tank. Perhaps most important to water quality in rearing marine tropicals at home is to make sure no chemical pollutants such as insecticides, paint fumes, tobacco, cleaning solutions, or other household contaminants get into the water. Such contaminants can create problems that are devastating in effect, yet extremely difficult to discover and eliminate.

Chapter 3

FILTRATION
Mechanical, Chemical, Biological and Sterilization

There are a lot of different things that can be done to aquarium water in the name of filtration, but they all fall under one of the four basic categories listed above. Your success as a marine aquarist will depend in great measure on how well you understand and work with the basic principles of biological filtration. The other types of filtration are important and helpful, but BIOLOGICAL FILTRATION is where all the action is. Without it you have a chemical time bomb, an engineer's nightmare and a pit of fishy despair sitting in your living room.

There are two basic types of contaminants in aquarium water—suspended, physical particles and dissolved chemical compounds. The physical particles may be as big as a baseball dropped into the tank by the kid next door or as small as a free floating bacterium. The dissolved chemical compounds may originate outside the tank from things such as insect spray or soap and perfume on the hands of an unwary aquarist, but except for these rare instances, dissolved contaminants are produced by the tank inhabitants. They are created from the metabolic waste materials of fish and invertebrates and also develop from the activity of bacteria on the waste organic matter produced in the tank. These dissolved chemical compounds include ammonia, nitrite, nitrate, urea, proteins, amines, fatty acids, phenols, dyes, and many other less abundant compounds. Briefly, this is what each type of filtration accomplishes in your aquarium.

MECHANICAL FILTRATION

Mechanical filtration removes suspended particulate matter. The efficiency of the filter depends on how fast water moves through the straining surfaces, the surface area of the filter and the size of the trap for the particles. A mechanical filter can utilize sand, gravel, floss, metal or plastic screens, or diatomaceous earth to strain particles from the water. Obviously, a filter for baseballs is designed and operates differently than a filter for bacteria. A mechanical filter usually also functions as a

21

biological filter if it operates long enough between cleanings. A good mechanical filter that removes very small particles with a rapid water flow is an excellent auxiliary to the basic biological filter because it maintains high water clarity, removes free swimming parasites, and removes accumulated dirt from the aquarium when it is cleaned. However, a separate mechanical filter is not an absolute necessity to a successful marine aquarium because the biological filter also acts as a mechanical filter.

CHEMICAL FILTRATION

Chemical filtration removes dissolved compounds and elements from the aquarium water solution. The four basic chemical filtration methods commonly applied to marine aquaria are: activated carbon, ion exchange resins, protein skimming (airstripping) and oxidation through ozonation. Activated carbon is able to remove dissolved organics from the water because each carbon grain contains uncountable microscopic pores throughout its entire mass. These tiny pores adsorb the molecules of various organic and inorganic substances from the solution and trap them so that they are no longer present in the solution. Of course the technical explanation is more complicated, but this gives you some idea of how activated carbon works. When all the pores are filled, the carbon is deactivated and functions only as a biological filter, but this takes quite some time depending on the filtering load. The home hobbyist really can't reactivate the carbon by baking it in an ordinary oven, except to drive off some adsorbed gasses, but if it is not exhausted, it can be cleaned of accumulated dirt and reused.

The adsorptive properties of activated carbon change as the carbon is used. New carbon has a greater ability to adsorb gasses than old carbon and, in general, will pick up more molecules at a faster rate. Some of the things that activated carbon will remove to some extent from your aquarium water are: oxygen and carbon dioxide (but not enough to effect a well aerated aquarium), copper, ozone, chlorine, many antibiotics, some dissolved proteins and carbohydrates, iodine, mercury, vanadium, chromium, cobalt, iron, molybdenum, methylene blue, malachite green, sulfa drugs, and organic dyes. Some of these are removed very quickly and efficiently, such as organic dyes, and others are removed slowly. Most compounds are not completely removed by activated carbon, but are reduced in concentration to variable extents. Thus, activated carbon is a mixed blessing to us aquarists because it pulls out a lot of good things as well as many of the nasties. It does not effectively remove ammonia, nitrite, or nitrate and can not substitute for a biological filter. Activated carbon can remain effective in home aquarium application for up to one year; and it may be that older carbon is better than new carbon because older carbon may retain the capacity to remove large organic molecules after its affinity for simpler compounds has diminished. Perhaps the greatest danger in using activated carbon is that it is so efficient in clearing and cleaning the water that it hides the need for occasional partial water changes.

Properly used, activated carbon can be one of the most useful tools of the marine aquarist. My opinions and recommendations on the general use of activated carbon are as follows. Set up the carbon filter as an outside power filter that can be turned off, removed, and cleaned without disturbing the tank. Use it very sparingly on invertebrate tanks because invertebrates seem to be more dependent on trace elements than fish. It can be used with frequency on fish tanks, especially older carbon, but give the tank frequent rests from carbon filtration, especially immediately after water changes or renewal of trace elements. Never use carbon filtration on treatment tanks or on a display tank during the rare occasions that you have to medicate the aquarium. Remember that no one really knows exactly all that activated carbon does or doesn't do to aquarium water, so use it cautiously and let your own experience be your guide.

Ion exchange resins are much more of an unknown than activated carbon. Opinions vary from advocation of certain resins as substitutes for biological filtration to total dismissal of any value to aquarists. To a greater degree than activated carbon, ion exchange resins can be manufactured to attract specific types of molecules. Some resins are utilized to remove ammonia or nitrate in fresh water sewage treatment and others are effective in removing dissolved organics. Some resins may give off small amounts of toxic chemicals and many are quickly confounded by the large number and type of free ions in salt water. I prefer to withold judgement and use of ion exchange resins in salt water systems until more information is available on their function and their effects on marine life support systems.

Protein skimming, airstripping and foam fractionation, all terms for the same basic process, is gaining in popularity as a water cleansing method for marine aquariums. The technique is old, but its application to marine aquariums is relatively new. Protein skimming operates on the principle that many of the compounds dissolved in salt water are attracted (adsorbed) to the interface (surface) between a gas and a liquid. Therefore, if you mix extremely tiny and abundant bubbles of air or other gas into a solution, many of the dissolved organic and some inorganic compounds will stick to the surface of the bubbles and ride them until they burst. When the organics are heavy, they coat the bubbles and create a surface foam, sort of like soap suds, but not as stable. Now if you can scoop up these suds and discard them, you can remove the compounds that stuck to the bubbles when they formed in the aquarium water. And this is just what the protein skimmer does, it collects the foam created in an airlift tube in a small cup above the tube where the foam breaks down into a nasty liquid containing all the compounds that stuck to the bubbles. This cup is emptied periodically and the aquarium is rid of many things like detergents, proteins, amino acids, dyes, fatty acids, albumin compounds, other organic compounds, and some inorganic compounds that tend to hook up with some organic molecules. However, there are problems. Like activated carbon, no one knows exactly what, and how much of it, is removed by an efficient protein skimmer and it is possible that valuable trace elements and nutrients are removed along with waste compounds. Also, protein skimmers have to be carefully adjusted for peak efficiency in a small marine system and if the air discharge is not at just the right volume and bubble size, the effectiveness of the unit declines greatly. Wooden air releasers, commonly used in protein skimmers because of the tiny bubbles they create, should be changed often for as the wood decays and fills with organics, air release is restricted. A protein skimmer can be a useful tool but you have to make sure that it is operating properly and remember that it may remove important trace elements and nutrients. The primary value of protein skimming and carbon filtration to the marine aquarist is that when properly employed, they significantly aid water clarity and cleanliness and decrease, but do not eliminate, the necessity of periodic water changes.

The last method of chemical filtration to discuss is oxidation of dissolved organics through application of ozone. Ozone is the triatomic form (O^3) of oxygen and is a very unstable compound. It is formed just before introduction into the water by air passing through an electric discharge. As the ozone breaks down in the water, it oxidizes or "burns" dissolved organics and kills bacteria and parasites. Ozone functions as a "chemical filtrant" in that it destroys dissolved organics if it is abundant enough and in contact for a long enough period of time, but it does not oxidize nitrogenous compounds beyond ammonia, so it can not substitute for a biological filter. In fact, it increases the need for biological filtration because it actually produces additional ammonia through oxidation of nitrate. The ozone contact tube should be of a counterflow design for maximum efficiency. This means that the water flow and the flow of ozonated air must go in opposite directions to insure maximum contact time of the ozone with the water. Ozonation is a delicate and dangerous filtration aid. Too much ozone escaping into the aquarium can burn the gills of the fish and cause death and distress, and not enough mixing with the water will not effectively oxidize the dissolved organics. Ozone escaping into the atmosphere can also cause headaches and stomach distress in humans, but there would have to be a great release of it before such symptoms appear. Each aquarium carries a different organic load and therefore requires a different amount of ozone, thus it is difficult to obtain maximum efficiency without delicate chemical adjustment. Activated carbon will pull out ozone and can be used to prevent a build up of ozone in the aquarium. Ozone is frequently used in protein skimmers and the efficiency of each is enhanced when they work together. Ozone treatment devices are best left to the advanced aquarist since they can create problems for the casual or unknowing hobbyist.

STERILIZATION

Sterilization can be considered a filtering method in that it removes life from the aquarium water. The most common sterilization device for marine aquaria is the ultraviolet light sterilizer in which the aquarium water is passed through a pipe that contains a short wave germicidal ultraviolet bulb. Some chemical filtration is also effected since the device also oxidizes dissolved organics. Other sterilizing devices release ozone into a contained tube of aquarium water and an ozone and air mixture. The ozone dissolves in the water and oxidizes the protoplasm of the target organisms. The primary use of sterilization devices is to decrease the abundance of free floating bacteria and control parasitic infections by destroying the organisms during the free swimming stages of their life cycles.

Ultraviolet light is a good sterilizing agent when the water is clear, the bulb is new, the UV has to penetrate less than an inch of water, and the exposure time of the water to the UV light is longer than one second. UV apparently works by affecting the function of the living cell by altering the structure of the cell's nuclear material and through production of ozone in the treated water.

The usual structure of a UV unit designed for marine aquarium use consists of a 4 to 8 watt UV germicidal bulb sealed in a watertight jacket that allows the aquarium water to circulate in a thin layer past the bulb. Both UV irradiation and ozonation have the capability to alter the structure of some dissolved chemical compounds. *Therefore, neither ozonation nor UV treatment should be used during treatment with any drug or chemical medication.* Sterilization of aquarium water is not necessary for maintenance of a successful marine tank. The most effective application for these devices is reducing the number of free floating bacteria and such bacteria are not a problem in a well maintained, uncrowded tank. However, if you feel that UV treatment helps to maintain a cleaner, more trouble free tank and that no problems can be traced to the unit, fine, but remember that the glass in the UV bulb will gradually change in its ability to transmit UV and it should be replaced every 8 to 10 months for the unit to retain its effectiveness.

BIOLOGICAL FILTRATION

Biological filtration is the transformation of toxic waste substances, primarily ammonia, into relatively non-toxic nutrients through the activity of living organisms, primarily nitrifying bacteria. Algaes utilize the nutrients produced by nitrifying bacteria, thus can function as a type of biological filter under the right conditions. Note that the phrase "removes from the system" is not mentioned in the definition of biological filtration as it is in the definitions of other types of filtration. The only drawback to biological filtration is that the process does not remove waste products from the aquarium, it only transforms the waste to compounds with very limited toxicity. These compounds accumulate in the aquarium and eventually have to be removed either through a complicated filtration system, or through the simple process of periodic, partial water changes. Marine aquariums can be maintained for years with only a simple, well aerated undergravel filter, monthly 10 to 25 percent water changes and semiannual filter cleanings.

Much has been said in recent literature about the nitrogen cycle, the "new tank syndrome" and nitrification and bacterial decomposition; and rightly so, for they all refer to the basic process that allows life to exist in your aquarium. Just as human communities need septic tanks or sewerage plants, aquariums require biological filtration. All animals, including fish, crabs, anemones, butterflies, snakes, and parakeets consume food and oxygen in order to grow new tissues and produce energy for living. Waste products in the form of carbon dioxide, undigested food and intestinal bacteria, and nitrogen wastes from utilization of protein and normal breakdown of body cells are produced by every animal and must be eliminated. The CO_2 content of the aquarium remains relatively stable despite constant production

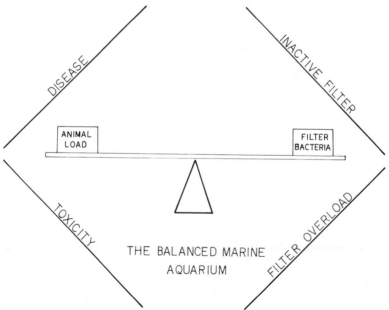

Figure 3. The balance of a marine aquarium. All is well as long as the activity of the filter bacteria transforms and neutralizes the wastes of the animal load. A tip in either direction creates problems for fish and invertebrates.

by animals and utilization by algae. Some of the CO_2 passes back and forth with the atmosphere depending on the condition of the aquarium. The remainder is either taken up by algae or enters the carbonic acid-bicarbonate-carbonate-hydrogen ions equilibrium, which is important with regard to the pH of the aquarium.

The solid wastes of fish and invertebrates, uneaten food, an occasional dead fish, and, rarely, an hors d'oeuvre all suffer the same degenerative fate. The aerobic (requiring oxygen) bacteria of decay attack this dead matter and produce, among other things, a lot of ammonia from the decomposed protein. This process of decay is termed ammonification. However, the major source of ammonia in a well run aquarium is from the nitrogenous wastes of the aquarium inhabitants. The way an animal rids itself of waste nitrogen depends greatly upon its relationship to water. Ammonia is rapidly formed in the blood of animals from the breakdown of protein and has the characteristics of being very toxic and very soluble. It must be either immediately excreted or rapidly transformed to a less toxic substance. Fish, living as they do in a watery environment, are able to excrete ammonia through their gills into the surrounding water. Land animals can not afford the water loss that would be the price of direct ammonia excretion and thus, through a clever biochemical mechanism known as the ornithine cycle, they convert ammonia to less toxic urea and excrete it in a concentrated solution whenever the mood strikes them. Some animals that live where there is very little free water, such as desert rats, are so conserving that they transform their nitrogenous waste to nontoxic crystals of uric acid that can be stored in the body or excreted in dry form.

Now we have a tank full of highly toxic, soluble ammonia derived from the activity of decay bacteria and animal excretion. Whatever shall we do? Fortunately, Mother Nature comes on like the U.S. Cavalry at this point with her nitrifying bacteria. These bacteria in the genera *Nitrosomonas* and *Nitrobacter* are found throughout the world and have the capacity to oxidize ammonia to nitrite, and nitrite to nitrate, respectively. All we need to provide is a surface for the bacteria to colonize and a source of ammonia. Even if we avoid a biological filter, which is only a device to provide a lot of surface area for bacterial growth, the bacteria colonize every available surface to do their oxidative work. The intermediate product, nitrite (NO_2), is also toxic, but less so than ammonia. Levels of up to 15 parts per million (ppm) can be tolerated by most species for a limited period. The end product, nitrate (NO_3), is relatively nontoxic and can be allowed to accumulate in the aquarium without much concern. However, if the tank is allowed to develop pockets of low oxygen or anaerobic conditions, bacterial reduction of nitrate can produce toxic compounds.

Ammonia occurs in two states depending on pH, the unionized state (NH_3) and the ionized state ($NH_3 {}^{+4}$). The unionized state is more toxic than the ionized state because it can invade body tissues more readily, but fortunately, almost all free ammonia is in the ionized state at the normal pH of sea water. As pH increases, the nontoxic form of ammonia rapidly decreases and the toxic form rapidly increases. Thus a lethal level of toxic ammonia may be present at a pH of 8.4, while the same total amount of ammonia may be tolerable at 7.8. Fish that are susceptible to ammonia poisoning may suddenly suffer symptoms if the pH increases rapidly when significant levels of ammonia are present. At any rate, levels of ammonia and nitrite should always be very near zero in the aged and balanced marine aquarium. The *Nitrosomas* bacteria are the first to populate the filter and rapidly begin oxidizing ammonia to nitrite. *Nitrobacter* is inhibited by the presence of ammonia and doesn't begin rapid population growth until after ammonia levels begin to fall.

Obviously these bacteria can not grow unless their nutrients, ammonia and nitrite, are present in the tank. They can be provided naturally by introducing some hardy fish and/or invertebrates or artificially by adding a solution of inorganic ammonia. This process is discussed in detail in the next chapter.

Great populations of bacteria must grow in the relatively sterile, new filter bed and it takes some time for such numbers to develop, especially if only a few bacteria are present at the start. Bacteria usually reproduce by division, one individual splitting into two, thus the last phase of population growth proceeds much more rapidly than the first phase. This is why ammonia and nitrite levels drop so rapidly to less than one or two ppm, usually within a day or two, even though they were building to high levels over a period of several weeks. Obviously, if we start out with a bacteria population of some size, the time required to establish the necessary nitrifying potential will be shortened because the initial period of slow population development is reduced proportionate to the size of the starting bacteria culture. In other words, the populations will increase faster if we start with two billion bacteria instead of two hundred. After the populations of *Nitrosomonas* and *Nitrobacter* are well established, oxidization of ammonia and nitrite occurs as these compounds are formed, thus they never accumulate in the system and only the end product, nitrate, can build to high levels. Nitrate can be removed by dilution through partial water changes or, since it is a basic plant nutrient, algae growth can prevent high concentrations.

The so called "natural system", a tank established without a filter, only an air stone or two to gently turn over the water, and containing a limited number of fish, invertebrates, and algaes, still depends on the same biological process of nitrification that the biological filter is designed to support and enhance. Nitrifying bacteria are still present and working hard but their populations are restricted to tank sides and most other surface areas present in the aquarium. Even such restricted sites for bacterial activity are sufficient if the tank is well maintained and the biological load is kept well within the range of natural balance. Invertebrates that consume waste matter and algaes that utilize nutrients greatly aid tank balance in a "natural system" aquarium, and their biological interaction is more important in this system since there is no efficient biological filter to provide a broad base of nitrifying potential.

Algaes can, and usually do, play an important role in the marine aquarium. They serve as a diet supplement for many fish and invertebrates, enhance the beauty of a natural tank and can perform as a biological and chemical filter. The type of algaes under discussion are the mixtures of single celled and filamentous green, brown, and red algaes that form on the sides and rocks of well lit aquariums. The brown algaes are usually the first to appear and are really diatoms or golden brown algaes. Heavy growths of these diatoms mixed with other algaes go by the esoteric name of "lab-lab" and are used in the culture of some marine food fish. Also included are the filamentous green algaes in the genus *Entromorpha*. These algaes form the thin, hair-like, green filaments that grow on rocks and glass and provide browse for many aquarium fish. Growth of the algae is dependent on intensity and quality of light and amount and type of dissolved nutrients. Diatoms and red algaes are most common in marine aquaria because they do not require relatively high intensities of natural spectrum lighting and are tolerant of less than optimum water quality. Good growths of green filamentous algaes are indicative of a well balanced, well lit marine tank.

Algae aid nitrification only in providing sites for growth of nitrifying bacteria. It is as a chemical filter that algaes really have potential. During photosynthesis (the process plants use to make food and energy from sunlight, water, CO_2 and nutrients) algaes take up CO_2, which keeps the pH of the aquarium high, and utilize nutrients such as nitrate that are made available by bacteria in the biological filter. Thus algaes can clean the water of accumulated nitrates, release oxygen, and remove CO_2; all good things to do for your aquarium. However, abundant algae growth will also remove trace elements and can be a potential disaster. As algal activity raises the pH, any ammonia present becomes more and more toxic as the amount of unionized ammonia (NH_3) increases. Usually ammonia levels are so low and algal activity so limited that no problems develop. Many algaes also use ammonia as a nutrient so ammonia seldom gets a chance to accumulate in systems with heavy algal activity. It is possible, however, for algal activity in closed systems under sunlight to raise pH levels to 8 and 9, so its worthwhile to be aware of the possibility.

There are delicate balances in a closed system aquarium between type and quality of algae growth, total animal load, quality and intensity of lighting, frequency and amount of water change, and degree of organic pollution (possibly from overfeeding). It is possible, especially in smaller, overcrowded tanks, to stimulate a luxuriant algae growth for several weeks or months only to have it suddenly die and pollute the tank. If heavy algae growths develop in the tank, the excess algae must be harvested and remaining growth closely watched for changes in type and amount of algae. The best situation is to grow just enough algae to supplement the fish's diet and help maintain a good quality environment, but not to the point where weekly harvesting is necessary. Placing the tank where it will receive a little natural sunlight each day will be a great help in achieving a natural balance.

Moderate algal growth in the tank is beneficial to the contained marine environment, but it can not properly be termed an algae filter. An external unit with algal growth controlled by harvesting and special illumination effectively serves to remove nitrates and CO_2 and performs a real filtering function. An algae filter is a worthwhile addition to an external compound filter that is sometimes used with large, 75 gallons and up, home installations built by skilled, advanced aquarists. The ultimate algae filter is a large, shallow, glass covered tray that receives natural

31

sunlight during most of the day and through which the aquarium water is continuously circulated. Care must be taken in such an installation, however, to avoid the extremes of temperature that can be developed.

A tank for rearing marine tropical fish larvae can have no bottom, figuratively speaking. The larvae of almost all marine fish exist only in the near surface waters of the sea where microscopic food organisms are plentiful and bottom growths with legions of predators are safely out of reach. Any type of filtration that collects tank water and directs it through a device that traps particles is bound to remove tiny food organisms and perhaps the larval fish themselves. Therefore, the easiest way to rear marine fish larvae is in a tank devoid of any filtration, at least during the first week or two, except for the nitrifying bacteria that colonize the tank sides and bottom. Sure, a filter can be developed that will circulate the water through a fine mesh with a large surface area, but except in the most unusual circumstances, it isn't worthwhile. A 50% water change each week during the larval rearing period (three or four weeks) is all that is necessary to maintain adequate water quality for most species.

Chapter 4

THE BIOLOGICAL FILTER
Function and Construction

FUNCTION

A biological filter is a living thing. It consumes oxygen, feeds on the waste products of animals in the system, and excretes wastes of its own. This is very important to remember for you must treat the filter as a living, breathing creature. The nitrifying bacteria in the filter are dependent on the oxygen contained in the water flowing through the filter. If this flow of oxygenated water stops, the good bacteria die, the water fouls, and the entire tank eventually dies. Because of this great demand for oxygen, there must be a rapid flow through the filter at all times. This is one of the major differences between the set up for a fresh water and a salt water aquarium. The amount of water flowing through a filter designed for a fresh water tank is not adequate for marine tanks and the proper populations of nitrifying bacteria will not be established. The best general rule for an undergravel, biological filter in a marine aquarium is to get the very maximum flow through the filter that your equipment can deliver.

The object behind establishing a biological filter is to bring the nitrifying capacity of the filter into an equilibrium with the waste production of the tank's inhabitants. The more efficient the filter, the more fish the tank can support. Each individual filter will have a maximum potential carrying capacity, which depends on many things beside the overall size of the filter. First of all, the amount of surface area of the filter is more important than the depth of the filter bed. This is because the bacteria need oxygen to do their work, and as the water flows through the filter bed, oxygen is depleted and nitrification decreases. Thus, the top ¾ inch of the filter bed does almost all the work. Other factors of importance are: the size and shape of the filter gravel, the rate of water flow, whether the filter is new and clean or old and dirty, and how the filter was established. The gravel size should be small enough to provide a large amount of surface area for a high bacteria population and to provide some mechanical filtration; yet large enough to allow a good water flow with some freedom from particulate clogging. Irregular gravel about 1/16 to 3/16

33

inch (1 to 4 mm) in diameter is a good size for a marine filter. It allows a lot of water to pass through and keeps the filter bed well oxygenated. Large air lift tubes at least ¾ inch internal diameter and a strong air flow broken up into small bubbles is essential to provide the necessary water flow through the filter bed.

A tank with no filter bed, such as a larval rearing tank or a tank set up according to the "natural method" (a few air stones, many invertebrates and a few fish) still develops a healthy community of nitrifying bacteria on every exposed surface inside the tank. Sand grains, shells, decorations, tank sides and algae growths all harbor colonies of nitrifying bacteria. So even a tank with no "biological filter" does, in fact, have a lot of biological filtering going on—it just isn't contained, isn't controlled and, quite often, isn't able to adjust to changes in tank populations or slight overfeeding. Larval tanks do not carry a large biomass, thus wastes do not quickly build up to toxic levels. Therefore, many fish can be reared in a relatively small tank with a few water changes during the four week larval period.

A filter bed established with an inorganic source of ammonia has a much greater initial carrying capacity than one started with an organic ammonia source such as fish or crabs. The reason for the increased carrying capacity is that all the available sites for bacteria growth are taken by the nitrifying bacteria rather than sharing sites with other types of bacteria that feed on other "foods" such as organic compounds. This allows large populations of the right bacteria to develop and the filter bed can operate at its maximum capacity. Ammonium chloride (NH_4Cl) is a good compound to use to establish the nitrifying bacteria with an inorganic ammonia source. Very little is required to develop the proper (1 to 5 ppm) concentration of ammonia in the tank water. You can fly by the seat of your pants and put in a tiny pinch for each 20 gallons or you can be scientific about it and add 10 drops of a 6% solution every two days for eight days. The important thing is to test the nitrite (NO_2) level in the tank at least every three days until the nitrite level has peaked, probably at about 15 ppm at 18 to 20 days after starting. It should then drop to less than 2 ppm; which should occur in 21 to 25 days. Many variables such as temperature, salinity, and type of substrate may extend or shorten this time period. After the nitrite level has dropped to less than 2 or 3 ppm, the tank is ready for fish and invertebrates. If water changes are no problem, a half change is very beneficial at this time and an innoculation of marine algaes, as a unicellular culture or a macroscopic plant, is also a good idea.

The chart on page 59 details the procedure for setting up and maintaining a marine aquarium with the organic and the inorganic methods of starting up along with a suggested care schedule for the first year. Not all aquariums will break in or run exactly by this suggested schedule, but this will give you some idea of typical marine aquarium maintenance.

OPERATION

Way back in the dark ages, the only biological filters commercially available were designed for fresh water aquariums and had only small diameter, big bubble air lift tubes to provide water flow through the filter bed. Therefore, the serious, knowledgeable marine aquarist had to build his own filter plate and air lift tubes to provide the kind of filtration necessary for a good

Figure 4. The structure and workings of the undergravel filter.

marine tank. Nowadays there are commercially available biological filters that are designed for marine aquariums and provide the proper construction features. If you purchase a filter, look for the three basic features a marine biological filter must have. We will assume that all commercially available filters are made from non toxic materials. First, the filter plate must fit snugly over the entire bottom of the tank and be designed to allow water to flow evenly through its entire surface. The plate should be positioned well above the bottom of the tank and allow water to flow evenly toward the bottoms of the air lift tubes. The plate should not allow the filter gravel to accumulate underneath and block off portions of the filter or restrict flow through the air lift tubes. Second, the air lift tubes should have an internal diameter of at least ¾ inch (2 centimeters), however, small tanks, 20 gallons or less, can get by with only ½ inch internal diameter. There should be an elbow on the air lift tubes at surface level to contain and direct the stream of water and air bubbles to various areas of the tank. Third, the filter material, (shell hash, oyster shell, silca sand, dolomite, quartz gravel, limestone gravel or any combination of these) must be of a particle size that allows free circulation of water yet still removes suspended particulate matter. A particle size of about 1/16 to 3/16 inch diameter (1 to 4 mm roughly) seems to do the job well. Particles this size do not cake up in certain areas and prevent water flow, but do filter out most suspended organic matter. All of the above mentioned materials will work well in a biological filter; but those of carbonate composition, coral gravel, oyster shell, dolomite or limestone also serve to chemically buffer the water and prevent the pH from falling to low. However, the buffering effect of these materials under average aquarium conditions is slight and will not prevent a drastic drop in pH in a crowded aquarium overloaded with organic matter. Filter bed material can be obtained at aquarium shops, plant nurseries and construction supply stores. Whatever the source and whatever the material, be sure to wash it well under running water until all dirt and organic material has been washed out. If oyster shell (obtainable from animal feed stores) is used, don't try to wash away all the milky water or the sun will set and rise on your efforts. In fact, even though the filter media is well washed, the tank water will be slightly milky for several hours to a whole day after set up until the suspended microscopic particles settle. These particles often settle on the glass sides and give the tank a cloudy appearance even though the water is clear. The sides can be easily wiped off if this occurs.

The filter bed also serves as a mechanical filter by removing suspended particles. Depending on their nature and the condition of the filter bed, these particles are trapped between the grains of filter media or become attached to each other and fill the larger spaces between filter grains. Eventually, the entire filter becomes clogged with organic material and the biological action of the filter declines. This detritus accumulates most rapidly in an overcrowded, overfed aquarium that receives a lot of light. A little detritus is good because it enhances the mechanical filtration and provides additional sites for nitrifying bacteria, but too much restricts water flow, cakes the filter bed, and enhances all bacterial growth. Thus the filter bed should be cleaned as required, usually about every 6 to 8 months, depending on the animal load. The depth of the filter bed is also important. The deeper the filter bed, the greater the mechanical filtration activity, the greater the build up of detritus, and the greater the risk of developing anerobic decay in the filter. Anerobic decay occurs when oxygenated water can not reach pockets of organic matter and then the bacteria that do not need oxygen go to work and produce hydrogen sulphide (that rotten egg smell) and other toxins that cause fish great distress. A filter bed depth of 2 to 3 inches is about right for most aquariums. This depth provides enough media for nitrification and mechanical filtration and gives the fish enough bottom to stir around without piling all the gravel up in one corner.

There are many techniques that can be developed for cleaning filter beds of accumulated detritus and undoubtedly you will develop the one that works best for you as you gain in experience. Aquariums that receive natural sunlight or intense artificial light and carry a heavy load of animals will accumulate detritus more rapidly than lightly stocked, sparingly fed tanks that receive minimum lighting. The basic idea, when cleaning time comes around, is to stir up the gravel to release the trapped detritus particles and then remove them from the aquarium. Filter cleaning and water changing can go together because the water removed when the bottom is siphoned can be replaced by new water. This is also a good time to give the entire tank a housecleaning, so I'll describe the whole process. It's not necessary to remove the fish from the tank unless you know from experience that they are hyperactive and will continue to bash themselves about the tank during the cleaning. Exposure to some turmoil and dirty water is usually less traumatic to the fish than capture with a net and removal to a holding tank. The first step is to remove any decorations that require cleaning. Some folks like their coral pieces and little castles to be free of green and brown algae growths and others prefer the natural growths. If these pieces can be cleaned with an old tooth brush and a little water, so much the better, however, if you must be clinical about it, a chlorine solution will quickly remove all organic growths. Be sure to wash off all traces of chlorine before replacing the decoration. The next step is to clean the sides of the aquarium of any heavy mats of algae growth. Unless a little algae interferes with the aesthetics of your ocean world, it is better for the inhabitants if you leave some algal growth on the sides that aren't used for viewing. The front glass is best cleaned with a plastic abrasive mat or sponge. Just don't carry the grease from last nights frying pan into your tank. The water will now be a little stirred up and the fish are looking for a safe place. A china cup or a rock that they can hide in, or near, gives them some security as their home is being cleaned. This temporary refuge can be moved from one side to the other as necessary. The detritus in the filter bed is much lighter than the gravel and will float up into the water as the gravel is stirred. The gravel can be stirred with a small rake or other implement, but fingers are best because you can feel and break up any caking of the filter material and have greater control over the stirring process. As your fingers work and stir the gravel, the detritus quickly clouds the water and then begins to settle out on top of the gravel. After the entire filter bed has been worked, the detritus must be removed. Much of it can be taken out by pulling a fine meshed net repeatedly through the water, but probably the best way is to let the dirt settle and then carefully siphon the accumulated detritus from the gravel surface. This removes the major portion of the dirt and a power filter can quickly pull out the remainder. Any gravel removed by the siphon can be washed and replaced, new salt water can then be added to replace that lost by siphoning, and the tank decorations then replaced. The water will clear in a few hours as the suspended particles that have not been removed settle out. This process will not kill the nitrifying capacity of the filter, but it will knock it back because some of the bacteria have been removed with the detritus and some have been dislodged from their sites. Keep a check on nitrite for a week or so after the cleaning to be sure that the tank readjusts properly and avoid adding new fish until everything is balanced again.

Filter cleaning is at best a time consuming, messy chore. It is possible to employ a full time automatic filter cleaner who'll be glad to work for what he can pick up on the tank bottom. A large marine hermit crab, *Pagurus sp.,* can gradually turn a filter bed over completely and consume uneated food, algae and some detritus and keep the bed loose and free for a long time. The detritus still has to be removed periodically, but Mr. Hermit Crab makes the job a whole lot easier.

CONSTRUCTION

It is possible to build an inexpensive filter plate and air lift system that will do a good job in a marine aquarium if you are a little handy with tools and are looking for a way to cut costs. Be sure all materials are nontoxic. Don't use metals or flexible vinyl plastics. Rigid, American made PVC pipe, available at most hardware stores is the best material for air lifts and filter plate supports.

The best material that I have found for a homemade filter plate is the plastic "eggcrate" used as a light diffuser for built-in fluorescent lights. This comes in 2 ' by 4 ' sheets and is available at do-it-yourself construction supply houses and electrical supply outlets. It is composed of vertical, half-inch white plastic strips molded to form a lattice of half inch squares. It can be cut with long nosed nippers or a hacksaw to conform to the shape of your tank. A piece of plastic window screening is cut to the shape of the eggcrate filter plate and attached with nylon string ties to prevent slipping. The plastic screening prevents the gravel from falling through the eggcrate and together they make up the basic filter plate. This plate must be kept up off the tank bottom about a half inch to allow free water circulation; this can be accomplished with small marbles regularly placed about the tank bottom or small sections of half inch PVC pipe about two inches long placed between the tank bottom and the filter plate. Whichever you use, be sure the filter plate is evenly supported and will not sag under the weight of the gravel and decorative pieces. The air lift tubes can be made from either ¾ or one inch PVC pipe cut to a length that will reach from the bottom of the tank to a point about ½ inch below the anticipated water surface. This will allow placement of a PVC elbow on top of the pipe to direct the flow of air and water. Many other air lift designs are available to im-

Figure 5. The elements of the homemade biological filter. The slotted ¾ inch PVC pipe sections support the filter plate above the tank bottom. The fiberglass window screen keeps the filter media above the filter plate and allows water to circulate through the entire filter bed. The air lift tubes bring water from beneath the filter bed to the surface of the aquarium providing water circulation through the filter media. The elbow joints on the top of the air lift tubes restrict spray and direct the water flow around the aquarium.

Figure 6. The construction of the biological filter. All the elements of the filter are in place. It is important for the filter plate to be well supported to prevent sag and possible breakage of the filter plate and screen.

Figure 7. The biological filter in place in the tank with the filter bed partially constructed. Note that there is a ½ inch gap between the filter plate and the front glass. The fiberglass window screening folds down in front of the filter plate allowing the filter bed media to fill this front space and hide the filter construction. Cut the screening with enough extra width to give this front edge plenty of support if this effect is desired.

aginative aquarists, and very decorative types can also be constructed if they function well. A good water flow about the tank is most beneficial to fish and invertebrates. Drill a 3/16 hole in the top of the elbow to allow the air line passage through the elbow to the bottom of the air lift tube. The air lift tube must project through the filter plate to the tank bottom. The easiest way to do this is to cut a circular hole in the screen and eggcrate that will allow the tube to be forced through the filter plate (it must fit tight to give support) and reach the tank bottom. Cut scallops or wedges out of the tube bottom to allow unrestricted water flow up the tube. Another method that requires more precision, but allows greater freedom in air lift placement, is to cut right angled slits in the tube bottom to allow the tube to slip over the cross in a one inch square of the eggcrate. This method also gives the strongest support of the air lift tube. The tube should reach all the way to the bottom of the tank and additional cuts should be made to allow good water flow. Use of a 1 inch internal diameter air lift tube will require careful cutting of a 1 inch diameter hole in the eggcrate or trimming of the tube bottom to fit within the 1 inch square.

The air stone should be positioned near the bottom of the air lift tube, but not so close to the bottom that air escapes from the tube and bubbles up through the filter media. Contrary to popular expression, water is pushed up the tube instead of lifted. When air is mixed with the water contained in the air lift tube, the mixture becomes lighter in weight than the water in the surrounding aquarium. This light weight mixture is then pushed to the surface through the tube by the denser, heavier water entering the tube bottom. Of course, once in the tube the new water is mixed with air and is in turn pushed to the surface where the air escapes and the water is recirculated. This is a very effective and efficient method of moving water around providing it doesn't have to be pushed very far above the surface. Now that we know how an air lift works its easy to see why very small bubbles of any given volume of air provide more push than large bubbles. The small bubbles rise more slowly, disperse more evenly and decrease the weight of the air-water column more than the release of large bubbles. Thus, the greater the weight difference, the more push and the more water flow. Wooden air diffusers create very fine bubbles and provide maximum push; however, they also clog and decay quickly so unless changing the air stone every two or three months is no problem, a high quality, fine bubble commercial air stone will give adequate service.

A marine aquarium can be a fantasy world under the sea complete with sunken boats, ceramic divers, plastic plants, fiberglass coral formations and fancy colored gravel. Or the aquarist may try to duplicate as natural an undersea setting as possible with algae growths, "living rocks", invertebrates and coral rubble. We should not belabor one extreme or the other for each represents individual creative efforts and provides satisfaction to the aquarist. However, if the creation of an undersea fantasy kingdom is your desire, be sure all the decor is safe for use in salt water. Colored gravel should be epoxy coated, or better yet, be composed of glass beads or chips, and plastic plants should not have metal weights or ties. Check manufacturers recommendations and make sure all aquarium decorations are marked as safe for marine use.

THE COMPOUND FILTER

Although an undergravel biological filter and a monthly to quarterly partial water change (10 to 20 percent) will maintain an uncrowded marine aquarium very nicely, advanced aquarists may decide to set up a separate water management filter system and circulate the water between the tank and a hidden filter bank. This is most worthwhile for a large installation, 75 gallons or more, but commercially available external power filters and other filter attachments can be used, if necessary, on smaller tanks as well. The water management system may be set up behind a wall or in a cabinet under the aquarium, and although a lot of work is involved in planning and building a custom-made filter bank, the best possible water quality and largest fish populations can be achieved. An aquarist advanced and skilled enough to construct a separate water management system will undoubtedly do a lot of research and experimentation and will have developed his own ideas on how it should be constructed.

Briefly, the elements that could be included in this type of filter bank, in order of the water flow from the tank through the filter, are: a mechanical filter, an algae filter, a protein skimmer, an activated charcoal filter, and an ultraviolet sterilzer. These would be in addition to the standard biological filter on the tank bottom. The system can be pressurized, except for the protein skimmer, and located below the water level of the aquarium. However, this type of unit is most difficult to service since it must be drained and taken apart to service and clean. A more functional design maintains the filter elements in unpressurized compartments at or above the tank water level. Each compartment should have an overflow, so if flow is restricted by clogging of one of the filter elements, the flow can bypass and not pump water out of the system. Also, if you build such a system, make sure the mechanical filter is easy to service, a simple floss replacement or washable foam pad works well. And if an algae filter is part of your system, grow the algae on a surface that can be removed, harvested and replaced; which is much easier than trying to scrape algae off the sides and partitions of an underwater box. Plan carefully, construct with quality and you'll have an efficient system.

OVERCROWDING

Don't overcrowd your tank! Everybody says that . . . I said that, but what does it mean? Essentially it means that the capacity of the filter bed and the tank water to maintain the existing animal load in good health is nearly exhausted. Of course, if the animal load exceeds the capacity of the system to process their wastes, then the tank balance is destroyed, bacteria populations

43

change drastically, oxygen decreases, toxins appear and fish die. This can happen suddenly; perhaps due to the introduction of a number of new fish into an already overcrowded tank; or more likely, as a slow breakdown when a well stocked tank is overfed and not maintained for many months. There should be a margin of safety, a buffer zone, between the maximum carrying capacity of the tank at any given time and the total animal load occupying the tank at that time. This safety margin allows for a skipped water change, an unobserved dead fish or a fish sitters overfeeding without danger of a tank breakdown.

So how do you know the safe carrying capacity of your tank? Unfortunately, this is one of those situations where the extremes are easily identified, a few fish in huge tank or dozens in a small one, but there is no precise line between too much and too little. There are so many variables that each individual aquarium set up has its own optimum carrying capacity, and this changes with age, maintenance schedule, and fish and algae growth. The filter bed is by far the most important single determinant of a tank's carrying capacity, however many other factors serve to extend or restrict the maximum animal load that can be supported by the system. The following list will give you an idea of the kinds of things that can limit the carrying capacity of your aquarium.

1. Filter bed too thin or too thick.
2. Filter bed gravel too small or too large.
3. Constricted or channeled flow through a caked up filter bed.
4. Filter bed heavily clogged with detritus.
5. No algal growth.
6. Consistent overfeeding.
7. Infrequent or no water changes.
8. Poor quality lighting.
9. Poor water flow due to small air lift tube, constricted air line or weak air or water pump.
10. Filter bed bacterial action inhibited because of medication.

The wastes and toxins produced by the animal load of a tank are balanced by the efficiency of the filter bed, the capacity of the water to retain altered wastes and still maintain life support quality, and the capacity of algal growth or supplemental filtration to extend the time frame of this balance. Thus, I can't tell you exactly how many fish to put in a certain size aquarium for a lot depends on how you set up and maintain your tank. However, I can give you a ballpark figure of 3 to 4 inches of fish per every 5 gallons, assuming that the tank has a full bottom filter bed and is not so high or so narrow that the filter area is unusually restricted, and suggest you watch for signs of overcrowding when this level of occupancy is attained. Some of these indicators of overcrowding are:

1. Reduction of green algae growth and more rapid growth of red and blue green algae.
2. Development of yellow water coloration before the next scheduled water change.
3. Persistent drop in pH below 7.8.
4. Rapid accumulation of nitrates and persistent traces of ammonia or nitrite.
5. Distress behavior in fish, fading colors, loss of appetite, hyperactivity, rapid respiration.

Some of these symptoms may have causes other than overcrowding, and if a water change doesn't help, then look for a very dirty filter and/or a disease problem. Remember, the most trouble free marine aquariums are those that are lightly populated with animals and have a moderate, stable growth of algae.

Chapter 5

PHYSICS AND CHEMISTRY
The Essential Information

Physics and Chemistry, two words that strike terror into the hearts of those who would rather stand in awe of the universe than dissect it. But don't worry, this section is designed to tell you in simple language only what you really need to know, so you can put away your calculator.

LIGHT

Light, its intensity, quality, and daily duration has great influence on all life and all environments and a marine aquarium is no exception. The major constant through ages of evolution has been sunlight. Temperature, water levels, and even continents changed, but sunlight was always constant and animals incorporated it into their essence as they evolved. They make vitamins with it, navigate by it, and among other things, control their reproductive periods by its daily duration. Too often we take light and the effects of light for granted, because it is always there at the flick of a switch and does not force our attention as does temperature. Yet because of its importance, we must take as much care to provide the right lighting as we do to provide the right temperature.

Sunlight in shallow tropic seas is very intense. The warm clear water allows some sunlight to penetrate hundreds of feet, although 80% of the sun's radiation is absorbed in the first 33 feet. Red, the long-wave end of the visible spectrum, is 90% absorbed in the first 15 feet, but blue and ultraviolet penetrate much deeper. Thus marine tropical fish from shallow coral reefs do best with relatively high light levels that contain at least the normal amount of blue and ultraviolet radiation. These short wave length radiations are particularly important for the growth of green algae and healthy fish. In fact, long-wave ultraviolet (black light) is said to have very beneficial effects on marine aquaria.

Under normal conditions, only fluorescent lighting should be used because incandescent bulbs produce too much heat. About 2 to 4 watts of natural spectrum (daylight) fluorescent light with a good reflector should be ample for a marine aquarium. This is roughly 2 tubes of the proper size for the length of the tank. It is a good idea to use an inexpensive timer to control the duration of light on the tank. Fish do best when the duration of light each day remains constant or changes very slowly. They should have 8 to 10 hours of darkness every day. Their periods of activity can also be controlled this way. Most aquarists prefer their fish to be active in the evening hours when they are home to enjoy them, so the timer can be set to turn the lights out at 11:00 PM and turn them on again at 7:00 or 8:00 AM. Fish adjust well to such a schedule and are less stressed than under a highly variable lighting schedule.

TEMPERATURE

All animals, with the exception of man who can engineer his environment, have a range of temperatures that define the limits of their existence. Their internal chemical reactions and external physical characteristics have adapted to particular environments through ages of evolution, thus polar bears aren't found in Florida and queen angelfish don't frequent New York Harbor. Fish, as all other poikilothermic (cold blooded) animals, are totally dependent on the proper environmental temperature range because they can not regulate their internal temperature. Lizards and snakes can bask in the sun to raise their body temperature or hide under a log to lower it, but fish can only be the same temperature as the water around them, so we must meet their temperature demands rather precisely.

The broad temperature range for most marine tropical fish and invertebrates is 65 °F to 90 °F. A few species can exist above and below these limits and a few have somewhat narrower tolerances. Please note that this does not mean that fish can be moved from 65 °F to 90 °F with one quick kerplunk. Fish can withstand rapid changes of a few degrees. I've seen such quick changes on the reefs due to varying current patterns, but slow changes are much easier on the fish. The extremes of the temperature range allow life only to survive. Optimum temperature for a marine aquarium ranges from 75 °F to 82 °F (24 °C to 28 °C). In these days of air conditioning, one seldom has to worry about tank temperatures rising above 85 °F, since heat loss from evaporation usually keeps the water a few degrees below room temperature. Tank temperatures can easily drop too low, however, and a good aquarium heater should be used to keep the tank at a comfortable, for the fish, 78 to 80 °F.

A heater can be very dangerous in a salt water tank because it produces heat through the electrical resistance of a wire coil, and if salt water gets into the heater it can be a very shocking experience. Glass immersion heaters with an internal thermostat are the most commonly used and are quite adequate providing they are designed for salt water use and have safeguards against intrusion of salt water and salt spray. An important safety measure is to unplug the heater while working about the tank. This prevents destuction of the heater through inadvertent lowering of the water level or removal of the heater while it is still active, since the glass tube quickly overheats and shatters if exposed to the air when the coil is heating. Be sure the heater is of the proper wattage for the gallonage of the tank. Too small a heater may not do the job when the room is cold and too large a heater can quickly "cook" a tank if the thermostat malfunctions. Figure the heater at about 2 to 4 watts per gallon or follow the manufacturer's instructions. Tank temperatures can easily creep up or drop without your noticing it if the heater malfunctions so be sure to have a water temperature thermometer always in or near the tank for ready reference.

SALINITY

Salinity is a measure of the quantity of inorganic solids (salts) that are dissolved in the water. It is usually measured in parts per thousand, ppt or $°/_{oo}$, and most tropical seas are 34 to 35 ppt (35 grams of salt in one kilogram of water). Coastal waters are often diluted by fresh water runoff and vary between 5 and 30 ppt. "That's easy to understand," you might be thinking, "But what's all this 1.025 S.G. stuff?" Well, this requires a little bit of an explanation. When three pounds of salt are dissolved in 10 gallons of water it disappears from view. The atoms of chlorine, sodium, and other elements that made up the white salts dissociate into their ionic states and slip in between the water molecules; and if the water didn't taste salty, you would never know they were there. There are other changes though, one of the most important is that a given volume of salt water is heavier than an equal volume of pure water. This means that an object is more buoyant (it floats higher) in salt water than in fresh water and the more salt in the water, the greater the object's buoyancy.

Specific gravity, S.G., is a ratio or comparison of the weight (density) of salt water, or any other substance, to the weight of an equal volume of pure distilled water. Thus, since 1 represents the value for distilled water, a heavier substance such as salt water will sink and has a S.G. greater than 1; and a lighter or less dense substance which floats has a S.G. less than 1.

Now our problem is to find out just how much salt is in the water and there are four commonly used methods to do this. In the traditional oceanographic research method, the quantity of chlorine ions (chlorinity) is measured by chemical analysis and the total salt content is calculated from this figure. Two other methods now commonly used are to measure the electrical conductivity of the water, which increases as the salt content increases, and to measure the refractive index (how light is bent by a thin film of water), which also changes with salt content. These methods are too complicated and expensive for most marine aquarists so the method of choice is to determine the specific gravity, a measure of density.

Since water gets denser as salt is added, we can determine its specific gravity by observing the relative buoyancy of a small glass float, and then determine how much salt is in the water by consulting a graph or table that converts S.G. to salinity. There is one variable, however, and that is temperature. Molecules of warm water are further apart than molecules of cold water because they have more energy and move faster. This means that warm water is less dense than cold water, thus a floating object sinks a little deeper in warm water. Therefore to get an accurate S.G. reading from a hydrometer, water temperature has to be considered.

A hydrometer is a weighted glass or plastic bulb with a calibrated stem that protrudes above the water surface. The hydrometer floats higher as the salt content of the water increases, thus S.G. can be read directly from the point where the calibrated stem is intersected by the water surface. The *meniscus* is the little upward curve the surface film makes as it tries to climb up the side of the glass stem. Take your reading at eye level from the flat surface of the water, not from the top of the *meniscus*, for greatest accuracy. Most hydrometers are calibrated to give an accurate S.G. reading at 59 °F (15 °C) although there are a few now that are made specifically for the marine aquarist and are calibrated at higher temperatures. Because of this temperature effect, a hydrometer calibrated at 59 °F and read at 80 °F will give a reading of about 1.022 at 34 to 35 ppt instead of the true S.G. value of 1.026. Translated into salinity, a true reading of 35 ppt will read 30.8 ppt at 80 °F on a hydrometer calibrated at 59 °F, so you can see that the temperature effect is significant.

BOX A — **BOX B** Observed S.G., hydrometer calibrated at 59°F (15°C)

ppt ‰	True S.G.	68.0 °F / 20 °C	69.8 / 21	71.6 / 22	73.4 / 23	75.2 / 24	77.0 / 25	78.8 / 26	80.6 / 27	82.0 / 28	84.2 / 29	86.0 °F / 30 °C
20	1.0145	1.0134	1.0132	1.0130	1.0127	1.0124	1.0121	1.0118	1.0115	1.0112	1.0109	1.0106
21	1.0153	1.0142	1.0140	1.0137	1.0135	1.0132	1.0129	1.0126	1.0123	1.0120	1.0116	1.0113
22	1.0160	1.0150	1.0147	1.0144	1.0142	1.0139	1.0137	1.0134	1.0130	1.0127	1.0124	1.0120
23	1.0168	1.0157	1.0155	1.0152	1.0150	1.0147	1.0144	1.0141	1.0138	1.0135	1.0132	1.0128
24	1.0175	1.0164	1.0162	1.0160	1.0156	1.0154	1.0151	1.0148	1.0145	1.0142	1.0139	1.0135
25	1.0183	1.0172	1.0170	1.0167	1.0165	1.0162	1.0159	1.0156	1.0153	1.0150	1.0146	1.0143
26	1.0191	1.0180	1.0176	1.0174	1.0172	1.0169	1.0166	1.0163	1.0160	1.0157	1.0154	1.0150
27	1.0198	1.0187	1.0185	1.0182	1.0180	1.0176	1.0174	1.0171	1.0168	1.0165	1.0162	1.0158
28	1.0206	1.0195	1.0192	1.0189	1.0186	1.0184	1.0182	1.0179	1.0175	1.0172	1.0168	1.0165
29	1.0214	1.0202	1.0200	1.0197	1.0195	1.0192	1.0189	1.0186	1.0183	1.0180	1.0175	1.0172
30	1.0222	1.0210	1.0208	1.0205	1.0202	1.0199	1.0196	1.0193	1.0190	1.0187	1.0184	1.0180
31	1.0229	1.0217	1.0215	1.0212	1.0209	1.0207	1.0204	1.0201	1.0198	1.0195	1.0192	1.0188
32	1.0237	1.0225	1.0222	1.0219	1.0217	1.0214	1.0211	1.0208	1.0205	1.0202	1.0198	1.0195
33	1.0245	1.0232	1.0230	1.0227	1.0225	1.0221	1.0218	1.0215	1.0212	1.0209	1.0205	1.0202
34	1.0252	1.0240	1.0238	1.0235	1.0232	1.0229	1.0226	1.0223	1.0220	1.0217	1.0214	1.0210
35	1.0260	1.0248	1.0245	1.0242	1.0240	1.0237	1.0234	1.0231	1.0228	1.0225	1.0221	1.0218
36	1.0268	1.0255	1.0253	1.0250	1.0247	1.0245	1.0242	1.0238	1.0235	1.0232	1.0228	1.0225
37	1.0275	1.0263	1.0260	1.0258	1.0255	1.0252	1.0249	1.0245	1.0242	1.0239	1.0236	1.0232
38	1.0283	1.0271	1.0268	1.0265	1.0262	1.0259	1.0256	1.0253	1.0250	1.0247	1.0244	1.0240
39	1.0291	1.0278	1.0275	1.0273	1.0270	1.0267	1.0264	1.0261	1.0258	1.0255	1.0251	1.0248
40	1.0299	1.0286	1.0284	1.0281	1.0278	1.0274	1.0271	1.0268	1.0265	1.0262	1.0258	1.0255

TABLE 1. CONVERSION OF SPECIFIC GRAVITY (SG) TO SALINITY (‰).

Table 1 on page 50 allows you to convert observed S.G. to true salinity quickly and easily. First write down the temperature and the S.G. reading from the tank or water sample. If the water temperature corresponds with the calibration temperature of the hydrometer, go directly to Box A and determine the salinity directly from the true = observed hydrometer reading. However, if the hydrometer is calibrated at 59 °F (15 °C) then go to Box B. Select the vertical temperature column that most nearly corresponds with the tank temperature, find the S.G. reading that is nearest your actual reading, and then move over horizontally on that line into Box A to determine the true S.G. and the correct salinity. If your observed S.G. value falls inbetween two listed values, you can achieve greater accuracy by interpolation.

In actual practice, you needn't get all in a dither about salinity. I don't think that the salinity of a marine aquarium must be any one particular value within a range of 28 to 35 ppt, (1.020 to 1.026). With the possible exception of certain invertebrates, marine animals and biological filters do better at salinities lower than oceanic sea water. Lower salinities keep more oxygen in the water, allow the nitrifying bacteria to work more efficiently, and reduce the metabolic work load of the fish. It is entirely possible to maintain a beautiful tropical marine aquarium at salinities of 20 to 25 ppt instead of 30 to 35 ppt. The only difficulty is the gradual acclimation of new fish to the lower salinities. Some fish are euryhaline and can move between salt and fresh water adjusting their osmoregulatory system to abrupt salinity changes. Most coral reef fish are stenohaline and must remain in sea water although they can adjust to lower salinities than those found on coral reefs.

All fish, fresh water or marine, carry salt levels in their blood and tissue of about 12 ppt, roughly equal to those of land animals. Fresh water fish do metabolic work to prevent loss of salt to the surrounding fresh water, and marine fish work even harder to prevent loss of fresh water from their bodies. Marine fish even drink sea water to increase their water content and excrete excess salt through special cells in their gills. Theoretically, lower salinities ease this metabolic work load and allow the fish to put this energy elsewhere. However, unless you want to do a lot of salinity response experimentation on fish and invertebrates, it is best to maintain your aquarium at salinities between 30 and 32 ppt. This slightly lower salinity does not increase acclimation stress on the fish and allows a comfortable evaporation margin.

Loss of ½ or 1 inch of water to evaporation will not push salinity up past the normal range. Be sure to put a mark outside the tank at the water surface right after filling it to the proper level. This allows you to add fresh water to replace evaporation loss without concern for salinity. If you must add a great deal of fresh water to make up for evaporation loss, do so gradually and avoid adding tap water heavy with chlorine or with a large temperature differential. Some salt may be lost through spray encrustation on the outer surface of the tank, but this is seldom enough to even detect through salinity measurements.

OXYGEN

The two things most essential for life in a marine aquarium are water and dissolved oxygen gas (O_2). Fish can live a short while without the other things, but without water and oxygen they die immediately. Dissolved oxygen is used by all the animals and the biological filter and is replenished almost entirely by oxygen entering through the air-water interface of the tank surface. Algae produces oxygen during lighted hours, sometimes a considerable amount if growth is heavy, but these same algae use oxygen during dark hours, so the gain is not completely positive, and oxygen levels quickly drop to normal saturation when algal photosynthesis stops. Some additional oxygen enters the water from air bubbles in air lifts, but this amount is quite small compared to oxygen entering through the surface. The tank water must be well circulated to maintain proper oxygen levels and this is one of the most important functions of the air lift system. Oxygen can not diffuse through water rapidly enough to replace that used by animals and filter bacteria, thus without good circulation, oxygen is quickly lost in lower levels of the tank. A tank can die after only a few hours without circulation through the filter.

Water does not hold a great deal of disolved oxygen and the amount it can hold decreases as temperature and salt content increase. Warm salt water holds about 6 to 7 ppm disolved oxygen. The activity of algae can supersaturate the water with oxygen and push it up to 8 to 12 ppm, but this is under unusual conditions. Most fish suffer severe stress when dissolved oxygen drops below 3.5 ppm and die when the level sinks below 2.5 ppm. Thus, in a tropical marine aquarium, there is only a difference of 2 or 3 ppm oxygen between a living tank and a mass of anerobic decay.

It is not necessary for the typical aquarist to measure oxygen levels, a rather complex procedure. But it is important to know that oxygen enters water very quickly and that normal oxygen levels are dependent on active water circulation throughout the tank. Also, the biological filter has a great need for oxygen and if circulation stops, the filter will quickly use up most of the oxygen in the lower levels of the tank. Watch for black discolorations in the filter and/or a "rotten egg" smell from anywhere in the tank. These are both sure signs that circulation is restricted and oxygen is being depleted in certain areas of the tank or filters. Another sure sign of oxygen depletion is if all the fish gasp at the surface and even try to jump from the tank. The latter is an extreme situation and would only occur under very crowded or dirty conditions when water circulation has completely ceased.

NITROGEN

Nitrogen and oxygen occur in the tank water bound up in numerous molecular compounds, nitrite (NO_2) for example, or as disolved gases. Nitrogen in the form of dissolved gas is not a consideration to the average marine aquarist. In some instances, water supersaturated with nitrogen and then compressed can cause "gas bubble" disease in small fish, but this seldom, if ever, occurs in home aquaria.

pH

One can be a successful marine aquarist without ever taking a pH reading, because if you go by the rules of good aquarium management, the pH of the tank water will take care of itself. However, the pH of your water is a good indicator of the quality of the environment you are providing for your finny friends and it is well worth knowing.

pH is a measure of acidity and alkalinity expressed on a scale of 1 through 14 with 1 being the most acid, 7 neutral, and 14 the most alkaline. The symbol pH stands for the "power of hydrogen" and the H is capitalized because it represents the chemical symbol of the element hydrogen. An acid condition is caused by an excess of the positively charged hydrogen ions (H+) and the alkaline condition is caused by an excess of the negatively charged hydroxyl ions (OH−); and when there is an equal number of each, the solution is neutral. pH is expressed on a logarithmic scale, each point being 10 times more concentrated

H + Concentration		pH	
10^0		0	
10^1	strongly acidic	1	——5% sulfuric acid
10^2		2	
10^3		3	——orange juice
10^4	weakly acidic	4	
10^5		5	
10^6		6	
10^7	neutral	7	——fresh water aquaria
10^8		8	——marine aquaria
10^9	weakly basic	9	
10^{10}		10	
10^{11}		11	
10^{12}		12	
10^{13}	strongly basic	13	——4% caustic soda
10^{14}		14	

TABLE 2.   THE pH SCALE (HYDROGEN ION CONCENTRATION).

than the one before. Table 2 gives a thumbnail sketch of the pH scale and lists a few common substances for comparison. Measuring pH is not at all difficult. It can be done with an electronic pH meter, with pH test paper, or with a liquid pH indicator. The latter two depend on color changes to indicate the correct pH. The liquid pH indicators are inexpensive and suit the needs of the typical aquarist very well.

The acceptable pH range for a marine aquarium is 7.6 to 8.3 and most well kept home aquaria fall between 7.8 and 8.1. There are a number of problems that can cause a drop in pH and if the water is filtered with activated carbon, these conditions may remain masked until the pH has fallen below 7.5. It becomes important to test pH if you do not change a percentage of water regularly and use activated carbon to maintain water clarity. A pH drop to less than 7.6 under these conditions indicates that it is past time for a water change.

Sea water has a considerable natural buffering capacity, that is the capability of picking up excess H + ions without lowering the pH value. However, the biological activity of the filter and the animals eventually overcomes this built in buffer and the pH begins to drop. The decline is hastened by overcrowding, heavy detritus accumulation, lack of exposed calcareous material and accumulation of dissolved organics. Regular partial water changes dilute H + accumulations and restore natural buffers. Sodium bicarbonate (baking soda) is frequently used to push pH up the alkalinity scale when water changes are not possible, but pH will drop again soon and water changes must be made eventually. If it becomes necessary to artificially buffer the tank to bring the pH up, it can be done as follows. Dissolve one teaspoon of sodium bicarbonate for each 20 gallons in a cup of water from the tank and slowly add the solution to the tank. Wait for thorough mixing to occur and then test pH. Do this repeatedly to bring the pH up to 8.0 and then test pH frequently until a water change can be accomplished.

The consistent trend in a marine aquarium is always toward a lower pH. Once in a while, however, pH can rise above 8.3, even to 9.0 in some cases. This is a result of CO_2 production by vigorous algal growth and is not in itself harmful; however, if such a high rise in pH is noted, it should be more than evident that the algae crop should be harvested.

DISSOLVED ORGANICS

Organic matter is added to the marine aquarium in the form of new animal or plant additions and as food for fish and invertebrates. This organic matter is cycled and recycled by the living organisms in the tank and eventually accumulates as either detritus or dissolved organics. Many organic compounds including proteins, amino acids, peptides, fatty acids, urea, ammonia, organic dyes, amines and phenols fall under the category of dissolved organics. Unless physically removed from tank through filter cleaning, algae harvesting, filtration and water changes; organics continue to accumulate and cause changes in the tank environment detrimental to its inhabitants. Excess organics accumulate slowly in uncrowded, sparsely fed tanks and rather quickly in heavily stocked, well fed tanks, but in either

55

case, they must be controlled by good aquarium management.

There are three sure signs of excess dissolved organics: a heavy persistent foam on the water surface, yellowish color to the water, and a drop in the pH. These become most evident if the maintenance routine has been skipped for two or three months and indicate a need for a filter cleaning and water change. Although partial water changes are the best way of controlling dissolved organics, they can be reduced to some extent by carbon filtration, protein skimming, and UV irradiation. New filtration products that claim removal of dissolved organics are appearing on the market, and if effective, should ease the life of a marine aquarist by extending the intervals between partial water changes. As with all new innovations, time will prove or disprove their utility.

Chapter 6

SET UP AND MAINTENANCE
The First Day, The First Year

The big day! You're ready to put together a marine aquarium. The following section should answer most of your questions and can serve as a basic guide during the first year of operation. First of all, watch your bottom. Most commercially manufactured tanks have a bottom supported with a plastic frame, but if this is not the case or if it is a large home made tank, be sure to set it up on a ½ to 1 inch thick sheet of styrofoam. This will even the stress on the bottom glass and prevent cracking. Position the filter plate and air lift tubes in the aquarium. Hook up the air stones in the tubes and make sure that they are about an inch off the bottom so all the air goes up the tube. Next spread the washed filter media to a depth of two to three inches over the filter plate. It can be a little deeper in some places than in others if you are trying to produce a special effect. Any decorations such as rocks, corals, and ceramics can now be put in place. These things are much easier to do before the water is in the tank and won't be disturbed when the water is added if it is done carefully.

If you do things the right way, the water is all made up, settled out, and ready to go into the aquarium. However, if you are the casual type, you may just pour the salt package into the aquarium and fill it with tap water. Although the latter method will work, it doesn't give you much control over salinity because a tank holds less than its listed gallon volume when rocks and filter media take up space. Place a china dinner plate on the bottom and pour the water into the tank on top of the plate. This will prevent the filter media from washing out of place. The plate is removed when the tank is full. Hook up the air pump and run the undergravel filter right away as this will help the tank to clear. Don't run any auxiliary power filters until the tank clears for this just puts unnecessary sediment in the filters. In fact, auxiliary power filters are not really helpful until after the tank has been conditioned or run in and has established its first balance between the filter bed bacteria and the animal load.

Be sure the tank has a close fitting, non-metalic cover. The cover should fit inside the edges of the tank to contain drips and condensation and prevent salt incrustations on the tank and table. A good cover also limits evaporation from the tank. The air in heated and air conditioned rooms is dry and will take up substantial quantities of water from an aquarium. The salt, of course, stays behind and salinity increases as the tank level drops. Make a mark on the tank side at the original water level and when the level drops about ½ inch, refill the tank with fresh water to the original level. *Never* replace evaporation losses with salt water for this just increases the total salt content of the tank water. Besides containing water and salt spray, a good cover prevents fish from jumping out of, and odds and ends from falling into, the tank.

The conditioning process can be enhanced by addition of "seed" bacteria from an already established tank. The advantages of seeding a tank with active filter media are first to introduce the proper kinds of bacteria and second to reduce the time required to build the proper bacteria populations. The disadvantages of this method is the possible introduction of disease organisms, both protozoans and bacteria. Seeding the new aquarium shortens the conditioning time by a week to 10 days depending on the amount of seed media used. Seeding is not worth the risk of disease introduction unless you are very sure that the source aquarium is healthy and disease free. Note that the time frames described below for tank conditioning are estimates and individual tanks can vary considerably depending on circumstances. Warm water and low salinity are two factors that will reduce the conditioning period.

It is now possible to purchase nitrifying bacteria in freeze dried form that can be added to the aquarium when it is first set up to provide a large dose of the right kind of bacteria. This does not give the tank an "instant balance", but if the product is good, it significantly decreases run-in time. An initial "food" is usually provided in the product, but it is still wise to start off with a few hardy fish until the nitrifying capacity of the tank is well established. One can also now buy bottled unicellular green algae cultures to add to new and established tanks to aid the growth of green algae. Some nitrifying bacteria are also introduced into a new tank with these cultures. Neither of these is a substitute for careful run-in and good aquarium maintenance, but they will aid the "balance" of the aquarium within the limits set by the condition of the individual aquarium.

Chemical testing for ammonia and nitrite are important during the conditioning period because it keeps you informed on the condition of the tank, and most important, it lets you know when the process is complete and the nitrifying bacteria are established. The ammonia test can be skipped if necessary because when nitrite (NO_2) levels rise you know that ammonia (NH_3) is being converted and that ammonia levels in the tank have dropped. Nitrite levels appear in the tank about day 10 and rise gradually to a peak of 20 to 30 ppm about day 20 to 25. The most toxic period for a new tank is the period from day 15 to day 25 when nitrite levels are at their peak. At some point, usually between day 24 and day 30, nitrite levels drop within a day or two to only 1 or 2 ppm. Thus testing for nitrite during the conditioning period tells you when the tank is most toxic and when the conditioning period is complete. It is possible to do the conditioning procedure even if you can't test for nitrite, but be sure to allow at least 40 days for run in before adding delicate and/or expensive species. An important point to remember is that a tank will not run in by itself. It must have an organic or inorganic source of ammonia to feed the developing bacteria populations. Keep a small notebook near your aquarium and make it a habit to record test results, water changes, algal growth, new acquisitions, spawnings and other events. This will take the guess work out of maintenance ("Lets see now, did I change water before or after Aunt Gert's visit?") and provide an interesting history of your aquarium.

TABLE 3. **CONDITIONING AND MAINTENANCE CHART**
FOR THE MARINE AQUARIUM

Time	Organic conditioning method	Inorganic conditioning method
Day 1	Set up tank. Run undergravel filter and allow tank to settle and clear. Add a cup of disease free seed media if available.	Set up tank. Run undergravel filter and allow tank to clear. Add ammonium chloride (NH_4Cl) to about 3 to 5 ppm. (A small pinch for each 20 gallons, or better yet, 10 drops per gallon of a 6% solution.) Add a cup of disease free active seed media if available.

Day 2	Wipe off any sediment that has settled on the sides. Add a source of organic waste matter. A couple of crabs or a few hardy and expendable fish will do fine. Feed sparingly.	Let it run and test ammonia if test kit is available.
Day 3	Feed sparingly twice a day, satisfy the animals but do not let uneaten food accumulate. Continue feeding throughout conditioning period. Note if appetite declines and then decrease the amount fed.	Add another dose of ammonium cloride.
Day 5	Continue animal maintenance. Test ammonia if kit is available.	Test ammonia if kit is available. Add another dose of ammonium cloride if ammonia levels are below 2 ppm. Skip dose if test is not made.
Day 7	Check ammonia and nitrite levels. Observe fish for signs of stress.	Add another dose of ammonium cloride if ammonia levels are below 2 ppm. Add a dose anyway if an ammonia test is not made. Begin to test for nitrite levels.
Day 10	Test nitrite level, it should begin to show up at levels of 3 to 10 ppm. Keep an eye on the fish for signs of stress.	Nitrite should show up now at levels of 5 to 10 ppm. Add a half dose of ammonium cloride and let it run. Check nitrite every other day until it peaks and drops to less than 3 ppm.
Day 15	Nitrite should be rising well above 10 ppm. Watch the fish and remove any dead or very distressed fish. Do not replace dead fish if nitrite levels are higher than 15 ppm.	Nitrite still rising. Should be above 10 ppm. Add a half dose of ammonium cloride.
Day 20	Same procedure as day 15. Nitrite levels should be near peak.	Nitrite should be near peak. Test levels every day if possible. This shows you when they begin to drop.
Day 25	If your fish aren't in stress yet, you know you have a hardy	Nitrite levels should fall off within the next 5 days, but may

species. Nitrite levels should peak and fall off within the next 5 days, although it's quite possible to run on another 10 days. remain high for a longer period in some situations.

Day 30 Most likely nitrite levels have peaked and fallen off to less than 2 or 3 ppm by this time for both methods of conditioning. If not, don't worry unless you want to, for nitrite levels will surely drop within the next 10 days. If temperatures are cold, below 75 °F, it may help to warm the tank up to 80 °F

Day 30 to 40 Begin the next phase as soon after the nitrite drop as possible, certainly within 5 days. Make a partial water change, 25% is about right at this time although you can go up to a total change if clean salt water is no problem. Now is the time to begin adding the fish and invertebrates you desire. Don't put in a great load all at once and begin with the specimens recommended as most tolerant of aquarium conditions. Add 1 or 2 animals to a 20 gallon tank and up to 5 or more in 50 gallons and up. Allow 7 to 10 days betwen each introduction of animals to let the tank adjust to each increase in the animal load.

Day 60 Time for a water change. Clean the front glass if necessary and remove any heavy build up of algae. Siphon out any accumulations of dirt that may be present on the bottom. Change 10 to 20 percent of the water with new salt water, either synthetic or treated natural salt water.

Day 90 Month 3 Repeat the maintenance performed at month 2. Change 20 to 25 percent of the water if you feel you have a heavy load of animals in the system. A 10 percent change is adequate if the tank is lightly populated. Make this procedure a monthly routine and you should have a trouble free tank.

Month 6, 7 or 8 Time for a filter cleaning (see chapter 4). It could come as early as month 6 or may drift to month 10 to 12 depending on lighting, animal load, feeding rates and invertebrate populations.

Year 1 Six to 8 months after the first filter cleaning your tank should be ready for another housecleaning. By now you probably have 2 or 3 marine aquariums and enough experience to write your own book, so good luck and give a helping hand to a fellow marine aquarist whenever you can.

TABLE 3. CONDITIONING AND MAINTENANCE CHART FOR THE MARINE AQUARIUM.

Chapter 7

FISH SELECTION
What to Look For, Condition and Compatibility

That healthy, alert, beautifully colored specimen in the tropical fish shop or a friend's tank had many rough times before it became adjusted to aquarium living. Unfortunately, collection, holding, shipping and distribution techniques are designed more for the convenience of humans than fish, and many fish arrive at their final destinations poisoned, stressed, diseased and starved. Many, perhaps most, of the marine fish that enter the trade do not survive more than a few weeks if they are captured on the reefs. This problem will diminish as more tank reared fish become available, but for now, we must live and work with the existing situation.

Acquiring new fish, either for an old aquarium or a new one, is fraught with anxiety and weighty considerations. Is this fish in good shape? Will he eat for me? Is that spot a scar or a parasite? Was he collected with drugs? Will he get along with the other fish in my tank? Will his coloration clash with my wallpaper? Most of these questions, and others like them, you have to answer for yourself. Your dealer may know some of the answers, but chances are he puts his faith in a wholesaler that has given him good fish in the past and doesn't know the history of each fish in his stock. One of the most important considerations, and one that I may be able to give you a little help with, is whether or not the fish is in good health. There are two basic areas for your evaluation: appearance and behavior.

When you judge the appearance of a prospective acquisition for your marine aquarium look closely at the eyes, mouth, skin and scales, abdomen, and fins. The eyes should be bright and clear and normally set in the head. Internal bacterial infections are often first seen in the eyes as a cloudy grey mist or in more advanced cases as an outward protusion of the eyeball. Sometimes only one eye is affected, and of course the fish keeps his good eye looking out at you, so be sure you observe both eyes when you evaluate the fish. Cloudy eyes and/or popeye can be treated, neomycin is usually effective, but you should know about it before you decide to buy him. A fish with sunken eyes, eyes that

62

seem too small for their sockets, is bad news, especially when the fish displays shallow respiration and little movement. This condition may be a result of exposure to a poison and his days are probably numbered. The mouth should open and close normally in respiration and feeding. Most species seldom open their mouths more than just slightly during normal respiration. A fish that keeps its mouth rather wide open all the time has problems that are hard to cure and is usually on a downhill ride. Respiration rates vary with species, age, and size; but extremely rapid gilling, except when the fish is upset by being chased with a net or fighting with other fish, is also a sign of trouble. Disease or parasitic infection (*Oodinium*) is the usual cause of rapid respiration, and the fish merits very careful evaluation when this condition is observed. The tissues of the mouth should be firm and uninjured. Mouth parts are often torn in fights with other fish and these torn tissues are potential sites for fungus and bacterial infections.

The skin and scales should be smooth and well colored. Indistinct, discolored blotches on the upper sides are usually a sign of an internal disease, especially when linked with rapid respiration. Uplifted or raised scales are also a bad symptom. Scales should be indistinct unless their edges are accentuated by the natural coloration of the fish. Missing scales are indications of fighting and are potential sites for infections. Fish are generally very hardy creatures and given a good environment and good nutrition, they can usually repair minor damage quite rapidly if they are not deeply stressed or diseased.

A fish usually stops eating when it is taken from its oceanic home and is subjected to crowded holding situations and unnatural foods. The period of starvation lasts until the fish encounters a wholesaler, retailer, or hobbyist that takes the pains to set him up in at least a semi-natural situation and offer food regularly until he begins to feed. During the period of starvation, the fish subsists on energy stored in its fats and liver and no great harm is done unless the fish goes without food past the point where the liver can recover. The abdomen or stomach area should be well rounded and slightly convex in profile in a healthy fish. As the fish loses condition, the abdominal profile becomes straight and then concave. In extreme cases, the stomach is pulled up almost to the spine, and the dorsal muscles are wasted and shallow. Needless to say, such a fish seldom recovers. The condition of the abdomen offers clues to the recent history of the fish and some indication of how easy it will be to get him to eat. Beware the sunken stomach.

The fins should be clear with smooth edges and the fish should extend them to their full spread with some frequency. Tightly clamped dorsal, anal, and pelvic fins are a sign of problems. Frayed fins indicate fighting or bacterial infections. Fins with frayed and bleeding edges and red spots have bacterial infections. If not checked, these will turn into open sores and invade the body, usually where the pelvic or pectoral fins touch the sides, and ulcers on the body will result. Oodinium is often first seen on the fins. The cysts on the body of a light colored fish might be overlooked, but the white pinpoints are noticeable on thin fins. A few oodinium cysts on a fish can be readily treated with a fresh water bath and a copper medication, but this parasite can quickly get out of hand and overrun a stressed fish in a few days. If one fish in a tank has oodinium, it's a sure bet that the others either have or will have the infection soon. If you spot oodinium in the tanks of a dealer, be sure to point it out to him for it can cause a dealer heavy losses of money and good will if allowed to progress unchecked.

Behavior is an important clue to the general health of the fish. It helps to know something of the normal behavior of your prospective fish, for then you can properly evaluate his (or her) actions. If the fish is normally nocturnal or secretive, then there's nothing wrong with hiding under a rock or in a corner. A fish of this persuasion, however, swimming slowly in the middle of the tank with fins clamped is in trouble. Conversely, a fish that normally swims about in the open waters above the reef should not hide continuously. Feeding is a very important sign of well being. If a fish feeds well on standard aquarium fare, the chances are that he is either in good condition or strong enough to shrug off any minor ailments. An active interest in his suroundings is also a good sign. The fish should respond quickly and actively to movements just outside and inside the tank. Although the term "bright eyed and bushy tailed" may not apply to fish, the basic concept does, so when you pick out your fish look for the ones that are bright eyed and full finned. A large part of the skill of a good marine aquarist lies in the selection of compatible fish that have the promise of surviving well in home aquariums.

COMPATIBILITY

There are perfectly good reasons why some fish are compatible in community aquariums and others are not; why some fish communities are peaceful and others are like a frontier bar on Saturday night. Unfortunately, there is no sure way of always knowing what behavioral interactions are going to occur between specific fishes in a particular aquarium situation.

The relationships between species that make up natural communities—not just fish but invertebrates, plants, and bacteria as well—have developed over millions and millions of years of living together and surviving to reproduce in a harsh and changing environment. Predator and prey, parasite and host, must coexist on the species level for each to survive. Each species must maintain its numbers within an optimum range, too many and the food supplies dwindle, too few and the reproductive effort is not adequate.

When we build a marine aquarium, the inhabitants we select bring along all their accumulated instinctive behavioral baggage—one of the things that makes a marine aquarium so fascinating and unpredictable. After all, a marine aquarium is like a multimillion piece jigsaw puzzle. All but a few pieces are missing, however, and the few that we have may not fit together just right, or in exactly the same way they did in nature.

In the vastness of the reef and nearby environs, there are species that seldom encounter each other, species whose separate instinctive methods of fulfilling their drives for food, protection and reproduction never bring them directly into competition with one another. Packed into an aquarium environment, however, they must now interact with each other as they compete for available food and space. The more active, mobile and aggressive species usually get the lionfish's share of attention, food, and occasionally, a tankmate. Some fish almost always can not co-exist with other fish in a small aquarium for one of two reason. They either feed so aggressively and actively on other fish that tankmates can find little shelter from them, or they are so docile and restrictive in food habits that most other fish easily outcompete them for food and space. Fish in these categories should be kept in tanks to themselves or with tankmates chosen by trial and error; and in these cases, experience is the best teacher.

Most of us do not choose to carry a study of species compatibility into the intricate web of coral reef ecology. We are content with knowing how certain species of fish and invertebrates commonly behave in marine aquariums, and how to expect, and thus avoid, loss and damage of valuable fish. To this end, it is helpful to have an understanding of why some fish are aggressive toward others.

The most important considerations in assessing compatibility are species, individual size, state of sexual maturity and activity, feeding habits, size of the aquarium, numbers of fish in each species group, and type and amount of habitat built into the aquarium. All these factors help determine the nature and intensity of aggressive behavior between aquarium inhabitants. Table 4 summarizes the kinds of aggressive interactions that can take place in marine aquariums.

The most obvious type of aggression is the predator/prey interaction. There is little question as to why a large grouper is aggressive toward a small damselfish. The interaction is quickly settled by the disappearance of the damselfish, either into the grouper or into the protective network of the coral reef. The aquarist uses this aggressive behavior pattern to good advantage when feeding guppies or mollies to a prize grouper or lionfish. Few aquarists are so naive as to expect the lion to lie down with the damsel in their aquarium. Most of the fish we keep in aquariums feed on smaller fish or invertebrates in the wild. Fish

TABLE 4. TYPES OF AGGRESSIVE BEHAVIOR IN THE MARINE AQUARIUM.

Type of Aggressive Interaction	Recipient of Aggressive Behavior	Example
Predator/Prey	Perceived food organism	Moray eel consuming a small clownfish
Territory Protection	Others of the same or similar species	Juvenile angelfish and jewelfish attacking others
Mate and Status Protection	Other fish of the same species	Paired clownfish attacking others
Spawn Protection	All other fish near nest area	Damselfish protecting spawn
Opportunistic Feeding Behavior	All other fish and invertebrates	Triggerfish

eating fish, except for sharks and barracuda, usually take their prey in one gulp so food organisms are seldom larger than a mouthful. Therefore, size differences are important considerations. A moray eel can co-exist with a large angelfish, but a small clownfish may only be a tasty tidbit. The three factors that work to the aquarist's advantage when keeping predatory and prey species in the same aquarium are size, familiarity and habitat. A small fish may co-exist with a large predator on a peaceful, if tenuous, basis for a long time simply because they both have a recognized habitat in the aquarium. The small fish avoids the predator and the well-fed predator is not stimulated to attack the familiar tankmate. Another small fish added to the aquarium is seldom so lucky. The predator's attention is drawn to the unfamiliar fish, the fright and anxiety behavior patterns displayed by the new fish arouse the feeding instincts of the predator and a strike is made. Under these conditions, the old time tankmate may also become a target, however, the old timer has a better chance of survival since it is familiar with the protective cover and behavior patterns in the aquarium.

Protective habitat, such as honeycombed rocks and coral growths that provide numerous safe havens, are necessary in tanks that hold groupers, lionfish, moray eels, and other predators as well as small reef fish. Even with the protection of extensive habitat and a good feeding program, however, small fish will occasionally disappear in such a situation. If one wishes to maintain a predator/prey relationship in a large tank, it is often helpful to separate the species with a partition of glass or transparent plastic for a week or so to allow the prey species to become acclimated to the tank and established in the mind of the predator. The reasons for other types of piscine aggression are not so obvious.

Proper habitat is the key to survival in nature. Although numbers of some species such as high-hats and cardinalfish can peacefully share a small habitat, others such as angelfish and some damselfish require some individual space. Each species requires a particular type of habitat to survive. Jewelfish require fire coral, clownfish require anemones, neon gobies must have large coral heads, high-hats need dark, intricate reef formations, small angelfish need sponges and crevices, and so it is with all fish species—some with broad and some with restricted habitat requirements. The fish that occupies, and holds onto, the right crevice, the right section of the reef where the proper food organisms occur, is the fish that will survive.

What would you do if you returned home one day and found a stranger fixing dinner in your kitchen with his suitcase in the bedroom. "Nice place you got here, buddy, I'm sure you won't mind if I move in for a while." With a little help from the police, I'm sure said stranger would soon find himself in different surroundings. In other words, you would aggressively remove the intruder from your private space. Individuals of many fish species protect their own living space (food sources, shelter and spawning sites) from others of their species in basically the same manner. A little queen angelfish may comfortably occupy the same crevice with a high-hat, blenny, a pair of gobies, a few cardinalfish and a puffer, but will not tolerate another queen angel within three feet. Other species do not compete for exactly the same resources as the queen and therefore are not a threat to its existence. These other species occupy different apartments in the same building, but another queen would be moving into the same apartment, not an acceptable living arrangement. The original owner has the power of occupancy — a power great enough to enable him to drive off even a slightly larger angelfish. When such an encounter takes place, a little nipping and posturing usually sends the intruder off to find an unoccupied apartment a few coral heads away. The angelfish may occupy this space for a few weeks or months until he outgrows the area and moves on to a new habitat more suitable to his size. Another small angelfish soon finds the deserted habitat and moves in, much to the delight of the tropical fish collector who has "staked out" that particular hole and collects a queen angel at the same spot every few months.

In the aquarium, the same instincts prevail even though there is no shortage of food or shelter. A territory is a territory and no other small angel is allowed within a certain distance. If this distance happens to be four feet and the aquarium is only three feet, then somebody has a problem, and it's usually the smaller of the two angels. In nature, the loser has a vast expanse of ocean bottom to escape into, but in an aquarium he is imprisoned with the owner of the territory. He can't fight back because he already lost the fight and the winner can't stop fighting because the loser won't go away. The result is either a dead fish or one that is so intimidated that he seldom ventures from a secluded hiding place.

Size is important to the intensity of intraspecific aggression. Often a large angelfish will tolerate a small fish of the same or closely related species because the size difference puts them in slightly different ecological niches and territorial aggression is muted. Another way of diffusing territorial aggression in an artificial situation is to contain many fish of the same size and species together, perhaps 20 to 200 or more in a relatively small tank. Aggression is then so diffuse, because there are so many fish, that no one fish can become dominant and no one fish can become the sole target for the aggression of all the others. All the fish give and take a little aggression and all survive. There is some indication that fish reared in such a situation are not as aggressive toward others of their own species as wild fish, however, this tendency probably disappears after the fish is kept alone for a period of time.

Young angelfish were used as an example of territorial aggression since it is often pronounced in these species and aquarists often try to keep them together, which is usually a mistake. Two small angelfish of the same species can seldom be kept together unless there is a significant size difference, and even in this situation, the smaller fish is barely tolerated and shows little or no growth. As a general rule, the more distantly related the species, the more tolerant they are of each other.

In certain families of marine fish, notably some species of angelfish and wrasses, a harem type of relationship exists between the sexes. One physically large male, often distinguished by color and form as well as size, maintains a territory with several to many females and aggressively protects his females from intrusion by other males. Some groupers may also exhibit this pattern in natural populations, but this is difficult to observe. It is interesting to note that protogynous hermaphroditism, functional females changing to males, is found in each of these, as well as other families of coral reef fishes. The loss of the male in these harem groups apparently stimulates a large female to begin to change into a male, which can take place within a matter of weeks. Behavior patterns change along with form, color and sexual organs.

An opposite pattern, protanderous hermaphroditism, occurs in anemonefish. In this case, one large, dominant female, a smaller male and a variable population of subadult fish inhabit a large anemone or area of anemones. The subadults are tolerated by the pair, but are kept in their place and they do not develop into adults. Upon loss of one of the pair, the largest subadult becomes an active male. If the female is lost, the active male changes to a female and pairs with the now maturing subadult male.

We are just beginning to investigate these fascinating physiological and behavioral changes that are apparently so common in coral reef fish. We have much yet to learn, much that will advance our understanding of how to care for these fish in aquariums. Development of aggressive behavior in a tank that has long been peaceful may be due to onset of sexual maturity or even sexual change. Individuals of some species protect their status within a sexual hierarchy as well as, or perhaps without regard for, a specific territory. For example, one male pigmy angel, *Centropyge,* may tolerate, interact, and even spawn with several females in a single aquarium; yet introduction of another male may cause intolerable aggression and loss of the new male. If the aquarium is large enough, however, a new female may fit into the harem and not cause undue problems. It is also possible for a small juvenile clownfish to occupy an anemone with a pair of the same species and suffer no more than an occasional nip; and if the relationship is well established, the juvenile will grow very slowly. A mature intruder into a tank with an established clownfish pair stands little chance of survival, unless it is so big and powerful that it can displace one of the pair. A female will be violently attacked by the resident female and a new male will be harried and picked upon by both male and female. It is possible to have 2 or perhaps 3 pairs each establish a territory in a large tank, but this usually happens only if the fish have grown up in the tank together. Once sexual maturity and subsequent pairing takes place in anemonefish, each mature fish protects its status by attacking all who might threaten this status.

Spawn protection is more intense and focused than status protection. This aggression is directed at all species of fish that venture near the nest. It only exists when a spawn is present or imminent. Damselfish and clownfish are most commonly observed protecting spawns since their nests are usually somewhat exposed. Royal grammas and neon gobies, on the other hand, are secretive spawners, their nests well hidden under a rock or in a crevice. Even though the nests are well hidden, an observant aquarist will notice the increased aggressive activity exhibited by the male near the entrance to his carefully guarded treasure. Many species we keep in aquariums become adults at relatively small size and form strong pair bonds between a male and female. Most commonly encountered in this category are some species of butterflyfish, gobies, clownfish, a few angelfish and, to a certain extent, royal grammas. These fish are often easier to keep as mated pairs than as singles, but when paired they seldom tolerate other fish of their own or similar species in the same aquarium.

Territorial protection is present in many species to a greater or lesser degree and usually results in loss or intimidation of one or more tankmates. There are some fish, however, that are so aggressive that few if any fish can be kept with them, and triggerfish are the prime example. They nip and bite the fins and body of all other fish kept in the same tank. This is not territory protection in the true sense, it is merely an aggressive, non-specific feeding behavior on a victim that can not avoid the slow swimming triggerfish because of the confines of the aquarium. Invertebrates are also subject to this never ending torment. This is just an extention of their behavior on the reef. They investigate anything that might be remotely edible with nips from their sharp teeth and small, but powerful, jaws. In fact, I once thought I had lost half an ear to a curious grey triggerfish one day as I was collecting angelfish. (Incidently, grey triggerfish fillets are good eating.) Triggerfish are among the most colorful and responsive of marine fish and are easy to keep, by themselves, in an aquarium. They are well worth a separate tank just to observe their behavior and beauty. Some triggerfish are said to recognize their owners and can even be taught to perform particular behavior patterns when food is offered.

Behavior patterns, developed over millions of years, that adapt a species to life in a particular ecological niche, do not fundamentally change when the fish is placed in the confines of an aquarium. The fish adapts to the aquarium only to the extent allowed by these innate behavioral patterns. Some species have behavioral characteristics that allow them to adapt to aquarium conditions quite well. The clownfish, for example, has a restricted range in nature, is active during the day, feeds on a wide variety of food organisms and is of small adult size; all characteristics that allow it to survive with vigor in a typical marine aquarium. The jackknife fish, on the other hand, is physiologically delicate and does not withstand capture and handling very well, it has a wide individual range in nature, and often will starve before taking typical aquarium foods. So despite its docile nature and spectacular form and color, it does not adapt well to life in captivity.

There are many pathways to survival. Some species have found that there is safety in numbers and interspecific competition for food and shelter has been reduced to the point that they can exist in groups or schools to the benefit of all the individuals. Surgeonfish, some damsels, grunts, jawfish (providing there is enough bottom area), cardinalfish, some wrasses and reef drums (high-hats) are examples of fish that form compatible living groups. Fish that live in groups or schools in nature usually get along well with themselves and other species in the aquarium environment.

The greatest compatibility problems usually occur when the aquarist brings home a valuable new prize acquisition to an old, established tank with fish that are well adapted to the tank and each other. Occasionally the new fish will be met with indifference, especially if it is a large fish that does not establish a particular territory or if the aquarium is relatively uncrowded. But more often, the old timers harass the newcomer unmercifully. There are several things the aquarist can do to ease the introduction process. New habitat, a rock or piece of coral added with the new fish may provide for the new arrival some cover unfamiliar to the established fish. Changing the position of all the tank cover is a bit more drastic, but it causes confusion in the established territories and allows the new fish to find a spot in the subsequent reestablishment of space claims. However, if the new fish is a large specimen of a species that is known to be aggressive, it is probably better to add it without any establishment aid since the old fish will be better able to maintain an already established position against a larger intruder. One of the best methods of bringing a new and delicate fish into an active community tank is to separate the new fish and a bit of habitat from the rest of the tank with a transparent piece of glass or plastic for about 10 days. This allows the old timers to see and accept the new fish before they can attack. It also allows the new fish to develop the behavior patterns of an established fish and defend its status when it does move into the tank's social structure.

Chapter 8

INTRODUCTION AND QUARANTINE
Purposes and Methods

Way back in 1864, Louis Pasteur proved that there is no such thing as spontaneous generation. Therefore, everything that shows up in your marine tank, except for air borne bacteria and perhaps algal spores, has got to be there because someone, somehow, put it there. This goes for disease organisms, copepods, parasites, and algae as well as fish, invertebrates and coral rock decor. Consequently, it is wise to stop and consider how things that you don't want, such as disease organisms and chemical toxins, could possibly get into your tank and what can be done to prevent their introduction. Remember that introduction of a nasty is not limited to the time of initial set up, indeed, this is the period when you are most concerned and aware and work hardest to avoid contamination. Slipups usually occur after a year of trouble free operation when you've developed the "Oh, I can throw anything in there and it does fine." attitude.

INTRODUCTIONS

We are most concerned with preventing the introduction of marine protozoan parasites *Oodinium* and *Cryptocaryon* and bacteria *Pseudomonas, Vibrio* and *Mycobacteria* since these organisms cause most of the disease problems in marine tanks. Although it is true that a healthy fish in a good environment can fight off a few bacteria, protozoan parasites are another story; they can quickly destroy a tank of fish if introduced and allowed to reproduce unchecked. The second concern (only because it is relatively uncommon) is the introduction of "unnatural" toxins such as nicotine, pesticides, rat poison, heavy metals, paint fumes and industrial chemicals. Anything that enters the tank has to be considered a possible source of contamination, especially if persistent problems are occuring, and the history of each routine introduction should be traced to make sure it is above suspicion. However, keep in mind that a marine tank is not an operating room and you need not try to keep it "clean and sterile." Indeed, that attitude could almost give one an ulcer. We are only interested in avoiding introductions from already contaminated marine sources or external poisons. Table 5 lists the most common modes of contamination and offers suggestions on prevention.

Table 5. Sources of Disease in a Marine Aquarium

Mode of Contamination	Methods of Prevention
Introduction of new salt water either as initial fill or as water changes.	Natural salt water should be treated (dark storage for two weeks) to prevent introduction of protozoan parasites. Synthetic salt water is safer, but be sure containers and hoses are rinsed with fresh water if they have recently held salt water from another source.
Introduction of active filter media when seeding a new tank.	The only precaution here is to know and trust your source.
Introduction of new fish and invertebrates.	Quarantine is the answer. See the following section.
Introduction of "living rock".	"Living rock" covered with attached invertebrates and algae can add much natural beauty and interest to a marine tank but, depending on the source, they can introduce protozoan parasites.. Quarantine for a week or so in a fish free tank is good insurance.
Fish and invertebrate food.	Every day food goes into your tank, and if you do a good job as an aquarist, the food is varied and from both plant and animal sources. Generally, any food that has been processed: freezing, cooking, drying, freeze drying, canned, etc. is free of parasite problems. The greatest danger comes from live foods: brine shrimp, plankton, live minnows, worms, etc., and dead unprocessed foods: shrimp,

74

fish flesh, algae are next in line. The answer is to be careful, but not paranoid. Know and trust your sources as well as possible. Don't introduce water that live foods are packed with and rinse well any unprocessed natural foods.

Introduction and transfer to coral, rocks or other decorations.	Make sure all coral or rock not intended to be alive is properly processed. Rinse and scrub well any transfers from possibly contaminated sources.
Introductions through nets, siphon hoses and cleaning implements.	It's easy to pick up a net, remove a dead fish from one tank, put down the net, then pick it up a few minutes later and use it in another tank. Get in the habit of rinsing all nets and cleaning materials in fresh water after each use and storing them in a dry place. Not only will they last longer, but possible parasite transfer will be prevented.
Introduction from air borne spray or splash over.	Aquarium set ups close to one another or over and under each other have the potential for spreading problems through drip and spray. Isolate the tanks as well as possible by space and covers and in the unfortunate instance that a tank develops a parasite problem, prevent any spray, splash or drip.
Introduction through casual or accidential means.	"Oh look Barbie, one of uncle Mike's fishies is on the floor. Lets put him in that tank over there. I wonder why he isn't swimming?". Good covers on tanks are important for obvious reasons. They keep fish in and little fingers out. The better your control over the tank environment, the less problem you'll have with accidents.

Table 5. Sources of disease in a marine aquarium.

The best preventative for protozoan parasite introduction, besides careful selection and a good dealer, is a one to two minute fresh water bath before introducing the fish to the tank. As long as the fresh water is the same temperature and close to the same pH as the tank water, the fish is only momentarily inconvenienced; but any external parasites not deeply imbedded in flesh or mucus quickly take up water until they burst from the increased internal osmotic pressure. If you also avoid introducing any of the water the fish were packed in, there is very little chance of contamination.

A good method of introduction; assuming the fish is not severely stressed, is in relatively good condition, and was packed under oxygen; is to float the packing bag unopened in the tank for about 15 minutes to allow temperatures to equalize. The bag is then opened and water from the tank equal to about one fourth the original volume is added to the bag. This allows the fish to gradually get used to the tank water and allows you to observe the fish's behavior as the tank water is introduced. If the fish becomes stressed when the tank water is added, something is wrong and the introduction process must be watched very carefully. Add the same volume of water about every 15 minutes three more times. Remove water from the bag and discard it before each addition of tank water to prevent the bag from filling. Now take a good look at the fish. If he is respiring very rapidly, listing to one side and in general looks very stressed, it's probably best to skip the fresh water bath and put him directly into the quarantine tank unless there are obvious evidences of parasite infection. However, if the fish is in good shape, a one minute fresh water bath is good insurance. Make sure the fresh water is the same temperature and close to the same pH (7.7 to 8.0 should be about right) as the tank water. Lift the fish with a clean net or hands and place him in the container of fresh water. Cover the container with something transparent if possible to keep the fish in and still let you observe. Time the bath and watch for signs of shock. If severe shock does occur, remove him from the fresh water bath and place him in the tank immediately. After one minute, put the fish in the tank and give him a day or two to settle down before critically observing behavior.

Other cleansing methods include use of copper compounds, medicinal dyes and antibiotics for periods of days or weeks before introduction to display tanks. Such treatments add to the stresses on the fish and are best avoided unless a disease becomes evident during the quarantine period or fish from a particular source consistently display disease.

QUARANTINE

The term quarantine can mean different things to different aquarists. To some, it's a sterile looking, medicated, bare tank that houses new fish for a day or two to see if any disease develops; and to others, it's a second fully set up smaller tank that maintains new beasties for several weeks to be sure all is well before introduction to the main tank. Both methods have their advantages and disadvantages. The bare tank allows effective use of medication, good observation of the fish, and opportunity to keep the tank bottom clean. However, the fish can not survive long or well in such a set up and the water should be discarded after each use. The bare tank finds its best application as a treatment tank, for use when a disease has been detected and a course of medication determined. A small tank, 10 to 15 gallons, set up with an undergravel, biological filter and a natural tank decor, is more functional for quarantine than a bare tank. It allows a new fish to be maintained under good aquarium conditions for two to four weeks to get used to the water, the tank routine and available foods away from the competition of the main tank. If a fish does bring a problem home with it, it should be evident within two or three weeks and, depending on the disease, treatment can be effected in the quarantine tank or in a bare treatment tank. A small quarantine tank is a lot easier to keep free of disease than a large display tank and can be used to brighten up another corner of the room. Following the simple procedures of selecting top quality fish, giving a one minute fresh water bath before introduction to the tank, providing a two week stay in natural type quarantine tank, feeding a varied diet, and adhering to a good maintenance schedule will give you a marine tank relatively free of death and disease.

Chapter 9

DISEASE AND DISTRESS
Identification and Cure

Suppose, despite your best efforts to avoid contamination, disease does strike. This is not an uncommon occurrence in marine aquaria and sooner or later every marine aquarist has to deal with a disease problem. This section is designed to help you identify the problem and suggest a method of treatment. However, disease diagnosis is an involved and complex subject, and although this section will help you cope with the most common problems a marine aquarist encounters, please be encouraged to seek other references and learn all you can about marine fish diseases and treatments. There are three steps to solving a disease problem.

1. Determining that a problem exists.
2. Identifying the cause of the disease or source of the distress.
3. Successfully curing the fish and eliminating the disease or cause of distress.

The first step, determining that a problem exists, may seem very simple—"Gee, when I got up and looked at my tank this morning, half the fish were dead and the rest were covered with little white spots." However, the trick is to catch the problem as soon as possible. The aquarist quoted above is actually saying that the first time in well over a week that he really looked at his fish, he discovered a problem that had been around for some time. Make it a point to observe the fish carefully at least every two or three days. Make sure they are all present, their behavior is normal, and there are no white spots, fuzzy skin, cloudy eyes, red fins or open sores. Behavior is often the best first indicator of disease, so watch for lack of feeding, listlessness, rubbing against rocks, color changes and other unusual behavior patterns. These are the things that tell you to look more closely and keep the tank under careful daily observation. The quicker a disease is identified, the better the chances for treatment and recovery.

Once you have determined that a problem exists, that things are not right with one, several, or all of your fish; the first thing to do is to stay calm and analyze the problem. Don't act until you are reasonably sure of the distress and have a carefully thought out plan of treatment. Treating a tank with a panicky dose of copper, for example, does nothing to cure a bacterial disease. Remember that the treatment can sometimes be worse than the disease so never rush blindly into treatment. Frequently, and especially in a neglected or overlooked situation, treatment will be complicated by the presence of two or more problems. An unchecked *Oodinium* infestation, for example, often leads to secondary bacterial infection through damaged skin and mucus layers and general stress. A fish weakened by harassment from other fish or poor environmental conditions is also a ready victim for bacterial disease. Keep in mind that certain basic problems such as bad environment and poor diet can be the underlying cause of continuing disease problems.

There are several important things to note and consider as you observe the fish. Consider the following questions and keep the answers generally in mind as you try to identify the cause of the problem.

1. How many fish and what species are affected?
2. When was the last water change and filter cleaning?
3. What are current ammonia and nitrite levels?
4. What is the tank water temperature?
5. What is the pH of the tank water?
6. How long ago was the newest fish introduced?
7. When was the tank last treated with copper, if at all, and is there any free copper left in the tank water?
8. How long has the distressed fish been in the aquarium?
9. What and how often do the fish eat?
10. Any past disease problems? If so, how long ago and due to what cause?
11. Any recent unusual introductions such as ornaments or chemicals?

Keeping a brief log book on your aquarium, as mentioned before, will easily provide answers to these questions and will increase your skill as a marine aquarist manyfold.

After you are sure that a problem is present (and hopefully you catch it so early that you can't be sure without careful observation) it must be identified and a course of treatment determined. It is difficult to prepare a check list or key to follow to ar-

79

rive at a specific cause of distress because many problems cause similar symptoms. Careful evaluation of the problem and attention to the following chart of ailments, Table 6, and discussion of symptoms and treatments, however, should enable you to cope with the majority of disease problems that may develop. The ailments are listed on the chart in the order of the frequency that they are likely to occur. This is a subjective arrangement based solely on my experience. The only reason for listing them in this order is to suggest to you which ailments seem to be most common. Another guide in the list is the check that indicates whether the ailment is usually common to all fish in the tank, fish of one closely related species group, or just one or two individuals in an otherwise healthy tank. Two checks indicate the most common circumstance even though it may also occur more broadly.

Descriptive term	Scientific term	all fish affected	one species affected	one or two fish affected
Oodinium Coral fish disease	Oodinium ocellatum	xx	x	
Cryptocaryon White spot disease	Cryptocaryon irritans	x	xx	x
Poor diet	Nutritional deficiency	x	xx	x
Poor environment		xx	x	

Toxins present
  generated within the tank
  introduced into the tank
		
		x
		xx
			
			xx
			x	

Harassment	lack of lebensraum			x

Fungus disease
  internal fungus
  external fungus
	
	Ichthyosporidium hoferi
	Saprolengia
		
		x
		
			x
			xx
				
				xx
				x

TB Fish tuberculosis	Mycobacteria marinum		x	xx

Bacterial disease
  Vibrio disease
  Pseudomonas
	
	Vibrio anquillarium
	Pseudomonas sp.
		
		x
		x
			
			x
			x
				
				xx
				xx

Viral disease Lymphocystis	Lymphocystis virus		x	xx
Fish fluke	Benedenia melleni	xx		x
Fish lice	Argulus sp.	xx		x
Old age				x

TABLE 6.   The Dirty Dozen Ailment Chart

SYMPTOMS AND TREATMENTS

This part of the disease and distress section provides basic information about the most common ailments, a description of the most obvious symptoms, and details of one or two treatments that, in my experience, usually effect a cure or solve the problem. The recommended treatments have been developed from a number of sources and many, if not most, are available in the pharmaceutical section of your favorite aquarium stores. Always read the ingredients and directions on aquarium pharmaceuticals and use as directed. Other medications can be obtained from drug stores, animal supply (feed) stores and scientific and chemical supply houses. There are usually a variety of effective treatments for each malady and I have tried to include the ones that are most effective and most available wherever possible.

Oodinium

Oodinium is also known as coral fish disease, white spot disease, and frequently as salt water ich. These secondary names for this disease are, in common usage, also applied to the protozoan disease *Cryptocaryon*. Beware of this confusion, because mistreatment can be the result. *Oodinium ocellatum* is a marine one celled alga, a member of the same group of organisms that cause red tides in marine waters. *Oodinium* does not cause red tides, but it is parasitic on fish during one stage of its life cycle; and in a closed system marine aquarium, this can be as devastating as a red tide. The reason *Oodinium* can be such a scourge is that, unlike some other marine pests, it can readily complete its life cycle in the aquarium and can quickly reach numbers that overwhelm the captive fishes. In nature, their numbers are kept in check by planktonic predators, dilution by ocean currents, movement of fish, and the cleaning activity of parasite pickers.

It is rare to encounter a fish in nature with a severe case of *Oodinium* parasitism, but on the other hand, fish with a few *Oodinium* cysts tucked away here and there are not rare at all. The life cycle of this parasite begins with the release from a mature cyst of 250 or more very tiny, free swimming cells called dinospores. The cyst is either trapped in the mucus of the host fish or has fallen off to the bottom of the tank. These free swimming dinospores seek out a host fish to obtain the nutrients needed for further development. The dinospores can not live long without finding a host. Some strains may not survive 48 hours, but others may last up to a month. High temperatures reduce the time that the dinospore can survive in the free swimming state.

The dinospore attaches to a host fish when it comes in contact with the external tissues of the host. Since fish are constantly pumping water through their gills, these soft respiratory tissues are the most frequent sites of infection. After attachment, the dinospore sends filaments into the tissues of the host to draw nutrients for its further development. After several days, the filaments are withdrawn and the parasite forms a cyst in which daughter cells develop into dynospores soon to be released and begin the cycle all over again. Depending on temperature, the life cycle of *Oodinium* is completed in 6 to 12 days. One or two of these parasites would have little effect on the fish, however, its easy to see that in a closed system aquarium this parasite can reach population levels that totally overwhelm any fish that may be present.

Symptoms: Oodinium infestations typically begin in the gills. Damage to the delicate gill tissue stimulates fish to produce excessive mucus in the gills and this condition restricts the exchange of respiratory gasses. The result is an increased respiratory pace (rapid gilling) which is usually the first outward sign of *Oodinium* infection. As the infestation progresses, the cysts become visible on the fin membranes and body surfaces. These cysts are about the same size and color as a grain of table salt and, especially on light colored fish, are difficult to see. They can usually be first observed on the clear fin membranes and show up best on the body when the fish is viewed lengthwise along its side. Infected fish often scratch their sides on the bottom or on rocks and sometimes shake or shudder while swimming. As the infestation progresses, colors fade, a powdery or dusty appearance becomes noticable as the cysts proliferate, and secondary bacterial infections often develop. Respiration is now very rapid and the fish begins to lie on its side on the bottom. It is usually too late at this point to save that particular fish, but some of its less infected tank mates may pull through if treatment is quickly provided. The time period between first observation of rapid respiration and terminal infestation may be as short as three to four days or may be two weeks or more depending on temperature, tank population and type and efficiency of filtration.

Treatment: A successful treatment for *Oodinium* consists of treating both the infected fish and the infected tank. If the parasite is not eradicated from the tank, reinfection will occur no matter how effectively the fish have been treated.

The most effective, no nonsense treatment for *Oodinium* is as follows. Prepare a fresh water bath of one to three gallons depending on the number of fish to be treated. Dechlorinate the tapwater if necessary by aerating it for several hours or add one small crystal of sodium thiosulfate or one drop per gallon of a weak solution of sodium thiosulfate. The pH of the fresh water should not be more than .3 points off that of the tank water. Add baking soda or a commercial buffer if the pH is too low. Remove the fish (all the fish) from the infected tank and give them a one to two minute bath in the bucket of fresh water. The fish can easily withstand the abrupt change in external osmotic pressure, but the parasites have no protection (unless they are deeply embedded in mucus) and quickly swell and burst. Thus the fresh water bath efficiently eliminates nearly all cysts on the fish as well as their potential offspring.

After the fresh water bath, the fish are placed in a treatment tank (5 to 10 gallons is a good size unless a large number of fish need treatment) with only an airstone for aeration and water circulation and some rocks or ceramics for fish shelters. Avoid coral, limestone and other calcareous objects since they tend to remove copper from the treatment water. Treatment for fish infected with *Oodinium* consists of three weeks exposure to a copper level of .2 to .3 ppm (parts per million) to destroy all dinospores that may be liberated before they can encyst on a fish, along with exposure to an antibiotic (neomycin, erythromycin or tetracycline) to control secondary bacterial infections. Refer to the bacterial disease treatment section for dosage.

If a level of .15 ppm copper can be maintained for two to three weeks, this is adequate to destroy *Oodinium* dinospores. However, this is the minimum effective level and it may not be adequate under normal aquarium conditions where proper levels of copper are difficult to maintain. Most fish are not harmed by levels up to .3 ppm, thus concentrations slightly higher than .15 provide a more sure cure.

Treatment of the fish is only half the cure. The *Oodinium* in the tank must also be eliminated. There are two ways to do this, both effective, and the best way for you depends on your own attitudes and methods. Time and temperature can be used together very effectively. Like all organisms with no internal temperature control, the *Oodinium* life cycle progresses faster at high temperatures because the chemical reactions of life take place more quickly. *Oodinium* also requires a host fish to survive. Therefore, the life cycle of the parasite can be broken if the hosts are removed and the process can be speeded up by increasing the temperature to 85 °F to 90 °F. All *Oodinium* cysts and dinospores can be eliminated from an aquarium in two weeks (three for sure) if the fish hosts are removed and temperature is elevated; and if the fish do not carry the parasite back with them when they are returned to the tank, the infestation is cured.

The second way is to treat the tank with copper. The most effective method is to remove any invertebrates and all calcareous objects. Treat the tank with a .3 ppm dose. Test the copper level the next day and elevate the dose back to .3. Wait two days, test the copper level again and bring it up to .25 if necessary. Thereafter, test copper levels every other day and maintain the dose at .2 to .25 for two to three weeks. The fish may be replaced in the tank after two to three days if necessary since the copper levels in the tank water will prevent reinfection. The copper concentrations must not be allowed to fall below .15 during the treatment period. After treatment, free copper in the tank water can be removed with activated carbon filtration and the invertebrates replaced after copper levels fall to near zero. However, once a tank is treated with copper there will always be some precipitated copper in the tank and the water should be tested before retreatment, especially if species sensitive to copper are kept.

There are shortcuts to this treatment method for the more casual aquarists that, although less precise, can be effective. The simplest method is to just dose the tank with a double dose of copper treatment (hopefully winding up with a .3 ppm level) at the first sign of *Oodinium,* add a second single dose two days later, another single dose three days later and hope that this will take care of the problem. It may, and then again it may not. The tank can be retreated whenever *Oodinium* is observed, for the presence of *Oodinium* is a good sign that copper levels are below .05 ppm. A fresh water bath for those fish most heavily infested will also be helpful. They can be returned to the tank immediately if the tank has been treated with copper. Such a shortcut is not good treatment technique, but its better than none as long as copper levels do not rise above .5 ppm.

Now a word or two about copper: Copper is not a cure all, in fact the primary, almost only, use of copper in the marine aquarium is to medicate for *Oodinium* infestations. This parasite is so common that without judicious use of copper treatments, keeping marine fish would be extremely difficult. There are, however, several problems inherent with the use of copper. First of all, it's a poison to fish as well as to *Oodinium*. The only reason we can use it is because it is slightly less toxic to fish than to dinoflagellates, and by carefully regulating the dose, we can wipe out the *Oodinium* and not injure the fish. The second problem is that it is difficult to maintain the proper level of free copper in an established marine aquarium. Many organisms, including bacteria and algae, and calcareous material remove copper from the water and can rapidly reduce its concentration below the effective level. However, repeated applications may quickly push the concentration into the toxic zone (.5 ppm and up) for fish. The third difficulty is that low levels of copper are quite toxic to many invertebrates such as anemones and coral and should never be used when these animals are in the tank. There is also evidence that copper treatment inhibits biological filtration to some extent.

Proper copper levels are relatively easy to maintain in a bare treatment tank if the copper solution is correctly prepared. There are many copper preparations available on the market today and most are compounded to deliver a .15 ppm concentration at a dose of one drop per gallon, but some deliver .25 ppm at the same dosage. It's important to know what concentration of copper is programmed to end up in the tank with a commercial preparation. The best way to find this out is to put a drop into a gallon of salt water or 10 drops into 10 gallons and test the resulting concentration with a copper test kit.

The copper in most commercial preparations is complexed, usually with an acid, to keep the copper in solution as long as possible. Other medications such as formalin are frequently added. Unfortunately, treating a marine aquarium with copper is not a simple, straight foreward operation. Even if you know precisely what concentration of copper the medication is designed to deliver, the tank may not be at all cooperative. Each aquarium set up has a certain capacity to pull out free copper from the water. Old tanks with a lot of detritus and calcarous material and infrequent past copper treatments can pull out much more copper than clean tanks with silica sand filters. It's possible to treat a tank with a full dose of copper only to have copper levels fall to almost zero in the space of a few hours. This is why it's important to test copper levels in the tank to make sure that the proper treatment level is maintained.

If you've a mind to, you can make up your own copper treatment solution. I'll give two formulas below, one for those with access to a laboratory type gram scale and metric volume measurements and one for those with only kitchen equipment and no other alternatives.

Dissolve 2.23 grams of copper sulphate (pentahydrate) and 1.5 grams of citric acid in one liter of fresh water to prepare the stock solution. Treatment with this stock solution at one milliliter per gallon of tank water results in a maximum concentration of .15 ppm. If the amount of copper sulphate and citric acid is doubled, the resulting solution will produce a concentration of .3 ppm at a dose of one ml per gallon.

If you are really stuck and can't get a commercial preparation and can't find someone to weigh out the chemicals for you on a gram scale and don't understand all this metric stuff

Figure 8. Copper sulphate and citric acid in the proper proportions to make three liters of copper treatment stock solution.

anyway, you can prepare a stock solution as follows. Copper sulphate and citric acid can usually be purchased at a drug store or a plant nursery. The copper sulphate should be in the form of small blue crystals (it's sometimes called bluestone) about 1/16th to 1/8th inch long (1 to 3 mm) Dissolve one level teaspoon of copper sulphate and one rounded half teaspoon of citric acid into three liters of fresh water. If you can't measure out three liters (100 ounces) use three quarts plus four ounces. A one gallon jug makes a good mixing and storage container for this stock solution. One milliliter (ml) of this stock solution per gallon of tank water should deliver about .3 ppm copper. There are about five ml per teaspoon (20 to 25 drops per ml), so one teaspoon of this solution for every ten gallons of tank water will produce about a .15 ppm concentration. Note that this method of preparation is quite inaccurate and there is a substantial risk of over or under treatment, especially if you do not test the aquarium water for copper concentration.

When adding any medication to your tank that calls for a certain dose per gallon, remember that there is more than just water in your tank. The undergravel filter and decorations, as well as fish, take up space that reduces the total volume of water. To determine how many gallons of water in the tank, multiply the length times the width times the height of water, all in inches, and divide the product by 231. This will give you the number of gallons that space will hold. Then deduct 10% or more, depending on the individual tank, to allow for the volume of the filter and the decorations.

Cryptocaryon

Cryptocaryosis is most commonly known as white spot disease and is also known as salt water ich. Inexperienced aquarists frequently confuse *Cryptocaryon* and *Oodinium*. It is quite different from *Oodinium* although there are many similarities. Like *Oodinium*, *Cryptocaryon* can complete its life cycle in a closed system aquarium and also has the capacity of overwhelming and destroying captive fish. The tomite is the motile infective stage of the life cycle. They are small ciliated protozoans about 50 microns long and their function is to find a host fish within a day or two or die in the attempt. Once they attach to the gill or body of a host, they develop into the second stage, the parasitic trophont. This stage burrows into the host and feeds on the host's tissues, often causing extensive damage. The well fed trophont eventually stops feeding and encysts, becoming the outwardly inactive tomont stage. This final stage may stay trapped in the mucus of the fish or may fall off and drift to the bottom. Within 6 to 10 days, hundreds of new tomites emerge from the tomont and seek another host fish to complete the cycle again.

Despite similarities in the life cycles, it has been my experience that *Cryptocaryon* does not overwhelm aquariums as rapidly as *Oodinium.* Perhaps fish have a greater natural resistance to *Cryptocaryon,* although the individual trophonts of *Cryptocaryon* seem to inflict greater damage than single *Oodinium* dinospores.

Symptoms: Although *Cryptocaryon* frequently infects the gills and causes respiratory distress, the first sign of the disease is usually several to a dozen white spots on the body and fins of the host fish. These spots are about the size of a pinhead and look very much like a small single pimple. The fish do not have the "dusted" or "salted" appearance that characterizes a severe case of *Oodinium,* unless of course, both parasites are present. These discrete white pustules become more numerous as the disease progresses. The gills become clogged with tomonts, mucus, and tissue debris. Bacterial infections invade the lesions caused by the trophonts and the fish declines rapidly. Scratching on the bottom or on rocks is a common symptom. Loss of color also occurs in patches or blotches as the erosion of the trophonts destroys pigment cells.

Treatment: As with *Oodinium,* the fish and the tank must be successfully treated to eliminate *Cryptocaryon* infestation. There are several methods of treatment that generally give good results. Unfortunately, copper is not as effective against *Cryptocaryon* as it is for *Oodinium,* although it does reduce the free swimming tomite stage; so other medications are needed. The first step in treatment is a fresh water bath since this will explode all trophonts and tomonts on the surface of the fish. This is not as effective as with *Oodinium* because *Cryptocaryon* burrows deeply and is protected by mucus and tissue.

The traditional treatment for *Cryptocaryon* consists of a one hour formalin bath (½ hour for sensitive species) every other day for a total of three baths and a copper treatment for the aquarium (as described in the *Oodinium* section). In this case, the fish can be returned to the aquarium after each bath as it is also under treatment. If you do not wish to treat the tank with copper and plan to maintain the fish in a separate treatment tank with a light (.15 to .2 ppm) copper treatment, the tank can be cleansed of *Cryptocaryon* with a time-temperature treatment of 10 days at 85 °F. This period allows four to six days for all tomonts to release their tomites and at least three days for all tomites to die.

Prepare the formalin bath by adding one ml of formalin for each gallon of salt water in the bath (one teaspoon to five gallons). Aerate this preparation very actively because formalin tends to reduce oxygen saturation, and carefully time the hour of treatment. If signs of shock appear, terminate the bath immediately. Formalin is a commercial preparation of a 37 ° solution of formaldehyde gas. It is commonly available at drug stores and janitorial supply houses. Full strength formalin is potent stuff so don't inhale it or get it in your eyes or on your skin. Formalin works as a preservative (and poison) by denaturing protein. Proteins, as you know, are the basic building blocks of life, and formalin, figuratively speaking, rushes in and changes the arrangements of the blocks and binds them permanently together so that the chemical reactions of life can not take place. At very low exposure levels, formalin destroys the parasites without bothering the fish. It also does the same thing to most bacteria, thus a good dose can wreak havoc with a biological filter. Formalin breaks down over a period of weeks in solution so it stays in the aquarium for some time. It is a useful treatment tool for *Cryptocaryon, Oodinium*, external fungus, external bacteria, fish flukes and fish lice, but keep effective doses in a separate treatment tank or you may pickle organisms you don't want pickled.

A new treatment developed recently by Dr. Edward Kingsford works well on *Cryptocaryon*. This treatment uses the antimalaria drug, quinacrine hydrochloride at a dosage of 4 to 6 milligrams per gallon applied directly to the infected tank. Quinacrine can be obtained through chemical supply houses and occasionally at drug stores. The drug does not affect the biological filter, but is active against protozoans. It may also be detrimental to anemones and corals so these animals should be removed from the tank before treatment. Carbon filtration removes quinacrine so these filters should be taken off and flushed with fresh water to destroy any stray cysts before reuse. The treatment requires two doses of 4 to 6 milligrams of quinacrine hydrochloride spaced 24 hours apart applied to the infected tank. Light levels should be reduced during treatment. After 10 days, residual quinacrine can be removed by activated carbon filtration. A water change after treatment is also a good idea. This medication leaves a yellow stain in tissues of fish and invertebrates that gradually disappears.

Another somewhat less effective treatment for *Cryptocaryon* is a five day exposure to the dye malachite green. One or two drops per gallon of a 1% solution makes up the treatment bath. After four to five days in a treatment tank, the white spot disease should be gone.

Poor Diet

A diet that provides all the essential nutrients is necessary to keep marine fish in good health over a long period of time. Fish suffering from malnutrition become susceptible to many other maladies and although death may be caused by a specific disease, the underlying problem is a fish weakened by malnutrition. Except for starvation, nutritional deficiencies do not occur quickly. They are the result of habitual poor feeding practices and, unfortunately, many fish keepers do not expend the little bit of extra effort that would keep their fish well fed.

Underfeeding is a common problem. Most fish need to be fed at least once a day, twice is better. In nature, many fish, particularly plankton pickers and sponge and algae browsers, feed almost constantly during their active hours. In an aquarium, they can do very well on two or three feedings per day if the food provides their basic nutritional needs. Underfeeding becomes a problem when no one feeds the fish for days at a time and then, after a big argument about who's supposed to feed the fish, someone sprinkles a little dry flake food in the tank and then lets it go for another few days. Fish don't have to eat a lot to be healthy, but they do need the right foods on a consistent schedule.

Overfeeding is bad for the fish and bad for the tank, especially consistently overfeeding dry flake foods. There are some aquarists that can not pass a fish tank without feeding the fish a little sprinkle of food. This may make the fish feeder feel good, but it quickly overloads the fish and the tank. Small fish that consume too much flake food too often, have a tendency to bloat after feeding and become so bouyant that they have difficulty staying near the bottom. Feeding the same food week after week without change promotes underfeeding for those fish that don't or can't eat well on the offered fare, and nutritional deficiencies for fish that require a wide range of nutrients. Many species require vegetable matter, preferably algae, in the diet to provide roughage and the proper balance of nutrients. See the section on foods and feeding for a positive approach to marine fish feeding practices.

Symptoms: The symptoms of malnutrition are very much like, and often are, the symptoms of a variety of diseases. However, some of the things to watch for that may be attributable to dietary deficiencies are: a tendency to bloat after feeding; a sunken stomach; overall thinness, especially behind the head under the dorsal fin; fading colors; loss of color in blotchy areas; erosion of the skin behind the head, especially angelfish; and general listlessness.

Treatment: Provide a good diet. Refer to the foods and feeding section.

Poor Environment

The aquarium environment has been well discussed in other areas of the book, and obviously, a bad environment can have detrimental effects on the fish. Some of the most common problems are: a lack of the proper kind and intensity of light, inadequate circulation through the biological filter, high organic load (yellow water) and subsequent drop in pH, and high or low temperatures. Some of these maladjustments of the aquarium environment can cause ammonia and/or nitrite toxicity (discussed under toxins), but more often they lead to general debility and reduce the life span of the fish.

Symptoms: Fish subjected to a poor environment show a fading of color, often due to a whitish film over the body (which may be a touch of external fungus or excess mucus production or both), are very susceptible to bacterial infections, lack a strong interest in feeding, and may stay in one small area of the aquarium with little ranging movement.

91

Treatment: Check water chemistry, the filtration system, and physical factors (light, temperature, water flow, etc.) to make sure that all is well. If you still can't identify the cause of the problem, and if no disease is evident, make a ½ water change, clean all or part of the filter and watch the fish carefully for either improvement or the appearance of a disease problem.

Toxins

Fish toxins get into aquariums in one of two ways. They develop within a tank through natural biological processes or they are introduced from an external source. Since these are very different in cause and effect, they will be separately discussed.

Internally Generated Toxins

A poor environment can cause toxins such as ammonia, nitrite, phenol, cresol, hydrogen sulfide, indole, and skatol to develop in the tank. The latter three are the result of anaerobic (oxygen lacking) bacterial processes and are very odorous. They develop only when a dirty outside filter has been turned off for several days and then turned on without cleaning or flushing, or when an undergravel biological filter is so clogged that aerated water does not circulate through all or part of it. Both conditions show severe neglect by the aquarist. A good aquarist usually discovers the problem when toxin levels are still very low and contribute only to a generalized poor aquarium environment as discussed previously. However, sometimes things degrade quickly and toxins reach a level where they cause severe distress, and even death, before the aquarist is aware of their presence. The average marine aquarist may encounter two problems caused by internally generated toxins. These are ammonia and/or nitrite poisoning (the "new tank syndrome") and a sudden unexplainable loss of almost all fish in a healthy looking tank within 12 to 24 hours ("the wipe out").

The "wipe out" or "toxic tank syndrome" is not a particularly uncommon occurrence, but it is very misunderstood and the effects are usually attributed to a disease. The syndrome most often occurs in tanks heavily populated with young fish of a single species, although it can occur in any type of marine closed system. The water is often very clear and uncolored with no trace

92

of ammonia or nitrite; and it usually has an acceptable pH when the syndrome occurs. My experimentation has shown that a virulent toxin is released from the biological filter and is often species specific, especially when numerous young fish of one species are present. Possibly a substance released from the fish stimulates the filter bacteria (not necessarily nitrifying bacteria) to produce a toxic substance or perhaps a new type of toxin producing bacteria are stimulated into a population bloom. Fish showing early symptoms of the toxic tank syndrome that are removed and placed in a totally different system almost invariably recover, and those left in the affected system almost inevitably die. Laboratory investigations showed that neither ammonia/nitrite levels or *Oodinium* are present. Total water changes slow, but do not stop the syndrome.

Although I knew that tanks of fish were occasionally mysteriously "wiped out" from time to time, it was always easy to put the blame on many possibilities such as tobacco, insecticide, *Oodinium*, bacterial disease or anything else that could cause such mortality. The specific nature and apparent source of the "toxic tank syndrome" was not apparent to me until I began to work with large numbers of young, tank reared fish in closed systems. Extensive work with very large numbers of small fish in small closed systems enabled us to identify the symptoms of this syndrome and subsequently trace the cause to a toxin released from the biological filter. It is possible that this toxin can be removed by chemical filtration, however, very little is known about it and much additional research needs to be done.

Symptoms: Ammonia/nitrite poisoning leads rapidly into bacterial disease because of the impaired functioning of the kidneys and liver. Excessive mucus is also produced in the gills and rapid respiration is one of the first signs of ammonia/nitrite toxicity. (If a water test shows no ammonia or nitrite, suspect *Oodinium*.) The fish may also keep their mouths open and move restlessly about the tank. In extreme cases, movement is rapid and the fish may try to jump from the tank, eventually colors fade, eyes get dull and the fish goes into shock and dies.

The "toxic tank syndrome" progresses very rapidly. As little as six hours may pass between onset and death, but usually 24 to 30 hours pass before its all over. Only the most virulent of bacterial diseases or severe poisoning destroys fish this rapidly. Only a few fish out of several hundred survive this syndrome.

The early symptoms are very rapid, shallow respiration and shimmy-like swimming movements that keep the fish active, but do not move him about. There also seems to be tremendous weight loss, especially in small fish, that gives them an emaciated appearance overnight. Possibly the biological mechanisms that maintain osmotic barriers break down and the fish lose body fluids to the surrounding salt water. Young fish also tend to group in schools facing the water flow and shimmy and shake almost in formation. Unless removed from the system, the fish soon lie on the bottom and die.

Treatment: Note that a high pH, 8.3 to 8.5, increases the toxicity of ammonia. If your fish show signs of ammonia poisoning and the pH is high for some reason, lowering the pH will bring the fish some relief. This would be a rather unusual occurrence, however, for pH in a marine aquarium rarely rises above 8.0 to 8.2 unless there is a great deal of algal growth, and if there is, the algae keeps ammonia levels low. Ammonia/nitrite poisoning usually occurs during the early life of the aquarium before the nitrifying bacteria are established or when the activity of the bacteria are repressed by medication, especially antibiotics, or after filter removal or cleaning. The best treatment is removal of the fish to a balanced, ammonia/nitrite free environment. If this is not possible, remove the most severely affected fish (or the most valuable) to an aerated bucket or unfiltered tank for several days until the ammonia/nitrite levels drop in the display tank. Add one ml per gallon of a 1% by weight methylene blue solution to the holding water to aid respiration and provide a mild medicant against fungus problems. Leaving ammonia/nitrite sensitive fish in an unbalanced tank, even with a water change, is usually a death sentence. The only real cure is to allow the tank to build the nitrifying bacteria population levels necessary to balance the animal load in the tank.

Persistent toxicity problems with newly made synthetic sea water may be the result of a new water treatment process for municipal water supplies. This process binds ammonia and chlorine in a stable compound that remains in the water despite typical treatments to remove chlorine from tap water. See Chapter II for a description of the problem and its remedy.

Fish suffering from the initial symptoms of the "toxic tank syndrome" present a little different situation. Usually the only way to save the fish is immediate transfer to another totally separate system. Water changes slow the progress of the syndrome, but do not prevent its reoccurance 24 to 48 hours later. There are two methods of treating the tank for this syndrome. Thye first is a good filter cleaning and water change and 5 to 10 days "rest" from fish occupation. The tank should be watched carefully for the next several weeks to catch any reoccurance. It is wise to change the species composition of the tank after a bout with a wipe out for the tank may become "sensitized" to a particular species group.

The second method is sterilization of the entire system, tank, filter and decorations; and reestablishment of the biological filter. Entirely new bacterial populations develop and any "sensitivity" to any species group is destroyed. Tank sterilization is probably the best thing to do if two or three "wipe outs" occur within a six to nine month period. See the end of the disease and distress section for details on tank sterilization.

Externally Introduced Toxins

Outside poisons seldom find their way into a tank, but when they do, they create many difficult problems. There are three ways such poisons can get into a tank: 1. on or in something the aquarist introduces into the tank, 2. an accidental introduction, and 3. Sabotage! A poison strong enough to, cause death and distress was probably introduced within a few days, or more likely, within a few hours of the onset of the symptoms. If you suspect a poison from an external source, review everything done to the tank within the last three days. Suspect new ornaments, new food, new water, and any unusual introductions. Remove these if possible and investigate carefully. Under number 2, review who had access to the tank (did your three year old nephew put moth balls from the closet into the tank?) Were there any recent paint or chemical fumes, any cigar butts or olives after a party? How about the most obvious, a zealous insecticide sprayer working behind and under the tank in the vicinity of the air pump intake? Number 3, sabotage, is another problem altogether, and if you worry about it, you're either paranoid or you've got problems way beyond the scope of this book.

Symptoms: Severe poisoning is very evident from the behavior of the fish. In most instances, there is violent swimming about the tank mixed with moments of rapid, heavy respiration. Fish will frequently jump from the tank, shudder and shake, and finally convulse and die. When this happens to all the fish in the tank, you know something is bad wrong. Perhaps worse than this though, is the mild case of poisoning that gradually kills the fish off one by one and is difficult to distinguish from the effects of a disease. The only way to separate these symptoms from those of disease is to note that the fish do not respond to treatment, that a disease can not be demonstrated, and that new fish always come down with the same symptoms. If this is the case, it's time to look for a possible cause of subtle poisoning.

Treatment: Obviously, the first step is to find and remove the source of the poisoning. Once again, the value of keeping a note book on aquarium activities is very evident. This will help you track down the time of new introductions, food changes and other things that may indicate the source of the problem. A good filter cleaning and a water change should put the tank back in shape once the problem has been corrected. Sterilization of the tank is a drastic step and should be a last resort.

Harrassment

Harrassment can be outright destruction of one or two fish in a tank or subtle repression of a fish into a hole or corner. Most reef dwelling fish require a certain amount of space between themselves and other fish of the same or closely related species. This territory that an individual or a pair establish and protect insures the fish of noncompetitive feeding, shelter, and reproductive areas and prevents pair bond confusion. This is a most complex and variable aspect of the study of reef fish ecology and new findings and concepts are frequently published. The study of fish in aquariums can provide insight into fish behavior patterns as long as the artificiality of the environment is understood. Harassment of one fish by others to the point of death or severe repression most commonly occurs when a new fish is introduced into an aquarium where a fish of the same or closely related species has already established a territory. If that territory includes the entire tank, the new fish is harassed until he is destroyed. In nature, the loser in such an encounter would quickly move on to an unoccupied area to find "lebensraum" or living space. However, in the aquarium there is no place to go and harassment continues until the intruder is dead. If the tank is large enough for more than one territory for that species, then the new fish may find a scrap of bottom or a hole to call his own. Although the fish can exist in this situation, he takes his life in his own fins when he ventures forth, and is always quickly chased back to his own area.

Territorial defense is usually not as keen in young fish and seems to break down altogether if large numbers of one species are confined in a small space. Intraspecific aggression can develop into harassment in a static tank if a number of young fish are kept until they grow larger and pair bond formation begins. This can happen abruptly or gradually as two fish, usually clownfish or damselfish, begin to repel others of their own or closely related species.

Symptoms: Harassment is usually obvious. In severe instances, the harassed fish is physically damaged with fins frayed and scales lost, and is usually found cowering in an upper corner of the tank respiring rapidly. The aggressor also respires rapidly and moves restlessly about the tank with quick aggressive attacks on the hapless intruder. The behavior of the fish and initial absence of bacterial infection in the wounds, easily distinguishes aggressive interactions from disease.

Treatment: Removal of the harassed fish or partitioning of the tank to separate the fish is the only treatment for incompatible tankmates. After separation, the injured fish should recover on his own unless he is badly chewed up, but watch and make sure that bacterial infection does not set in. It may be necessary to isolate the injured fish in a treatment tank with an antibiotic treatment.

Fungus Diseases

Fungus diseases in fish, especially internal infections, are not uncommon and are very difficult, if not impossible, to cure. Fortunately, fish have natural resistance to fungus disease and if a healthy environment low in dissolved organics and good nutrition are provided, fungus infections are rarely a problem.

Internal fungus infections are caused by *Ichthyosporidium hoferi*, a parasitic fungus in the class Phycomycetes. This fungus is not detectable until the advanced stage of the disease causes degenerative changes in behavior and appearance. Unfortunately, there is no positive cure. Many fish seem to be able to contain and control this parasite and evidently live many years with this tiny parasitic time bomb ticking away inside their vital organs. Stress and poor nutrition may weaken the defenses of the fish and release the fungus to destroy the spleen, liver, brain and other organs.

External fungus infections are caused by organisms in the genus *Saprolegnia*. These are visible as cotton-like tufts about the mouth or as a thin whitish coating on the sides of the fish. The appearance of external fungus usually indicates that there is an underlying problem, either nutritional or environmental, that should be corrected.

Symptoms: Symptoms of internal fungus infections do not appear until the disease is well advanced. Loss of appetite and listlessness are the first symptoms as the fungus proliferates in the liver and kidneys. Dark nodules under the skin may appear along with areas of upraised scales. The infection soon passes to the nervous system and causes exothalmus (popeye) and loss of equilibrium. The fish swims in random circles often swimming upside down. The abdomen may also fill with fluid and be distended. There is nothing that can be done for a fish in the later stages of this disease. External fungus infections do not destroy the life function of the fish and are easier to deal with. *Saprolegnia* appears as cottony tufts near the mouth or on the fins, occasionally growth about the mouth is great enough to obstruct feeding and can cause starvation. External fungus also occurs as a thin white coating on the sides of the fish. It can be easily distinguished from *Oodinium* because *Oodinium* occurs as discrete specks and fungus infections appear as a variable white film with thick and thin areas. Severe cases can erode the skin, introducing secondary bacterial invasion, which eventually enters the abdomen and destroys the fish.

Treatment: When it becomes obvious that a fish is infected with either internal or external fungus, there are two important concerns besides the infected fish. These are the health of the other fish in the tank and the tank environment. Fungus infections are very hard to treat and care must be taken to prevent it from spreading. A water change and, if necessary, a filter cleaning and increased dietary variety are the best preventative steps to take. Also, an effective UV water treatment unit is helpful in preventing the spread to other fishes. Usually only one or two fish show the symptoms of internal fungus disease and these should be isolated and given good water quality and good food. I know of no really effective medication and if the fish show no signs of improvement after a few days to a week, it is best to destroy them. Fungus is most often transmitted by healthy fish feeding on an infected dead fish or contaminated fish flesh. Remove dead or dying fish from aquariums immediately and be careful of feeding raw fish flesh.

A persistent case of external fungus may be treated by removing the fish from the tank, holding him carefully, and swabbing the fungus area with a cotton ball soaked in an iodine medication. Copper sulphate solution, malachite green solution and 2-phenoxyethanol can be applied in the same way, but these are all experimental procedures and could be worse for the fish than the external fungus. Given a good environment and good food, a fish can usually lick a mild case of external fungus by himself.

Fish Tuberculosis

Fish tuberculosis, piscine TB, is a wide spread marine fish disease caused by the bacterium *Mycobacteria marinum*. There are a number of species in this genus, including the one that causes TB in man. *M. marinum* does not commonly infect people, however, there are reports of serious skin infections caused by *M. marinum*. In these instances, the aquarists were cleaning tanks that had held TB infected fish and had either an open lesion or suffered a cut while working in the tank. The open lesions developed into abscesses that did not heal and after several weeks, additional abscesses developed on the hand and arm. These infections did not respond to penicillin and treatment was not effective until the antitubercular drugs isoniazid and streptomycin were given. This is a very rare human infection; but it can happen, so if you work with an open wound in a marine aquarium, be sure to disinfect the lesion very thoroughly. Penicillin doesn't work on *M. marinum* so if this does happen to you, tell your doctor that those nodules on your arm may be fish tuberculosis.

Fortunately, fish TB usually hits only one or two fish in a tank and the course of the disease is slow enough to allow time for treatment. Fish showing symptoms of TB should be isolated immediately, for although it is not highly contagious, it can lead to tank wide mortality. Contagion is especially likely if fish that die of TB are left in the tank and healthy fish pick at and consume the soft parts of the dead fish.

Symptoms: Piscine TB and internal fungus, *Ichthyosporidum*, have similar symptoms and can be confused. However, loss of equilibrium, swimming in circles, sideways and upside down, is not usually a symptom of piscine TB. The first symptoms are loss of appetite and general listlessness. The fish stays hidden and soon has no interest at all in feeding. Rapid respiration is usually noticed about this time also. The fish may remain in this stage of the disease for several weeks. The eyes may become clouded and exothalmus (popeye) usually develops. Another typical symptom is the development of whitish blotches and areas of raised scales. Finally the fins become ragged, the abdomen sunken, and the fish lies on its side on the bottom. The fish may linger in this state for many days before it dies. The internal organs of affected fish degenerate and small greyish granulomas are found on and in the liver, intestines, spleen and eyes. One type of piscine TB forms granulomas along the spine of young fish. These can sometimes be seen through the flesh as a whitish discoloration along the spine of small fish.

Treatment: Piscine TB is a difficult disease to treat because it is internal and the effective drugs are not easily obtained. Since there is a strong possibility that the average aquarist will not be able to obtain the proper drugs for treatment, the affected fish should be immediately isolated in a treatment tank to reduce the chances of infecting other fish. At the risk of sounding like a broken record, I must stress that piscine TB is most common in poorly maintained aquaria. A good environment and good nutrition keeps the natural immune system of the fish in top condition and practically eliminates the occurrence of piscine TB.

If the disease is caught in the early stages, treatment with streptomycin and isoniazid may effect a cure. Kingsford, in his recent book (see reference list) also recommends rifampin and cycloserine although these two may be difficult to obtain. Streptomycin may be found in some commercial aquarium medications or obtained at drug stores, veterinary supply and animal feed stores. Isoniazid can be obtained through chemical supply houses and, since it does not seem to affect nitrifying bacteria, it can be used in a tank with an active biological filter. Be sure to turn off all carbon and UV filtration before adding any medication.

Add 40 milligrams per gallon of isoniazid and 40 milligrams per gallon streptomycin to the treatment tank when the fish are transferred. Change water every three days, more often for small tanks and/or large fish, and remedicate. Add 40 mg per gallon of isoniazid to the display tank to reduce the chance of infection. Soaking the food in streptomycin solution or adding 6 mg of rifampin per 100 grams of food increases the effectiveness of the treatment. If medicated food is prepared, it should be fed to all fish that have been exposed to the disease. Return fish to the display tank when they have apparently recovered. Do not return a fish if there is any question of recovery for it is best to lose one or two rather than risk all other fish in the tank. If most of the fish in a tank come down with TB or if the disease persistently occurs in a particular tank, it is best to sterilize the tank and start again.

Bacterial Disease

The world is full of bacteria, indeed life as we know it could not exist without the activities of bacteria. Bacterology has become a very complex discipline involving the most advanced techniques of taxonomy, biochemistry, and microscopy. One of the basic taxonomic tools of bacterology was developed by the Danish physician Christian Gram in 1884. He discovered that bacteria could be separated into two groups depending on whether they retained (Gram-positive) or lost (Gram-negative) a violet color during a particular staining process. He didn't know it at the time, but this differential staining was caused by fundamental differences in the structure of the cell wall, which also affect the way antibiotics work on bacteria. Most bacteria that cause disease in marine fish are Gram-negative and some antibiotics, including penicillin, streptomycin and sulfa drugs are not effective. *Pseudomonas* and *Vibrio* are the genera of the principle disease producing bacteria in marine fish. The antibiotics neomycin, chloramphenicol, and secondly erythromycin and tetracycline are usually effective against these bacteria. There are other antibiotics that may be even more effective, but they are also more difficult to obtain. Some of the above antibiotics are frequently found in aquarium pharmaceuticals or in farm animal medications obtainable at feed stores.

Fish have a strong natural resistance to bacteria so infections caused by *Pseudomonas* and *Vibrio* seldom overrun a fish unless there is a stress and/or weakness already present in the fish. Old age, poor nutrition, poor environment, injury, harassment, fungus infection, etc. can all contribute to the debility that opens the door to bacterial disease. Occasionally, the environment is so poor that bacterial growth can bloom and overrun otherwise healthy fish. Cloudy water of a white, rather than green, hue and persistent sores on the fish are symptoms of this condition.

Symptoms: The most obvious symptoms of bacterial disease are reddened, frayed fins and open sores on the sides, usually near the fins. External ulcers are generally caused by *Pseudomonas* sp. and internal bacterial infections seem to be caused more often by *Vibrio* sp.

Usually only one or two fish in a tank at any one time show symptoms of advanced bacterial infection. If all fish are severely affected, then the aquarium is in bad shape and a major overhaul is required. Common symptoms of bacterial disease are rapid respiration, a grey film over the eyes, bloody scales at the base of the fins, disintegration of the fins and open sores on the body. Bacterial disease may also cause blindness in fish. Blindness is usually evidenced by cloudy eyes, failure to see their food or movements outside the tank, and lack of response to a net moved slowly toward them. Excessive light alone, if there is such a thing in a marine aquarium, does not cause blindness, although it could increase stress levels in nocturnal fish.

The lateral line system, that row of tiny pores extending along the side from head to tail, is the most frequent site of initial external infection. Bacteria can gain entry into a stressed fish through these tiny pores and the soft tissues of the gills. Internal organs are affected as the disease progresses; the fish stops eating, respiration rate increases, and eventually the fish lays on the bottom and dies. Some bacterial diseases may kill the fish in two to four days, but usually, especially in larger fish, the progression of the disease takes one or two weeks.

Treatment: Only the affected fish need be treated if the infection is restricted to one or two fish and the other fish and the environment appear healthy. However, if most of the fish show signs of bacterial infection, it may be best to treat all the fish and sterilize the tank. This will prevent frequent reoccurrences of the same problems during the months to come. The tank can not be treated with a strong dose of antibiotics without killing the nitrifying bacteria (they are also Gram-negative), so tank sterilization is best in the long run for a severe or persistent bacterial disease problem.

The infected fish should be isolated in a treatment tank. A fresh water bath (see *Oodinium* section) on the way to the treatment tank is a good idea in case there is a parasite problem, but it won't do much for a bacterial disease. Reduce light levels on the treatment tank to preserve the activity of the antibiotics and reduce stress on the fish. Add the antibiotic you choose to the treatment tank at the manufacturer's recommended dose. If there is no listed dose for aquarium fish, use neomycin at 250 mg per gallon, chloramphenicol sodium succinate (Chloromycetin) at 50 mg per gallon, tetracycline at 50 mg per gallon and erythromycin at 40 to 50 mg per gallon. Positive results should be noted within three to four days if the antibiotic is effective. If the treatment is not effective, try another antibiotic. Once the fish gets the upper hand over the infection, with the help of the antibiotic, recovery is rapid. Keep the fish in isolation until recovery is assured. Wait a day or two after ulcers are healed and eyes are no longer filmed before replacing them in the display tank. An effective UV sterilizer on the display tank will be helpful in preventing a build up of dangerous bacteria in the tank water.

Lymphocystis

This is the only viral disease that commonly affects marine tropical fish. It also goes by the name "cauliflower disease" because the appearance of the growth is not unlike that of a miniature cauliflower. The virus invades cells just under the skin of the fish, usually fins or lips are affected, and causes these cells to swell greatly (hypertrophy) and form a thickened cell membrane. These enlarged cells proliferate into a small growth with a characteristic form and color. The virus does not kill the fish directly, although the growths may interfere with feeding or may create a pathway for secondary bacterial infection. In many respects, lymphocystis is similar to a wart on humans. Given time and no secondary complications, fish will usually recover from lymphocystis infection on their own.

Symptoms: The fish displays small, discrete, gray or whitish growths on lips and/or fins. These growths may appear all over the body in a severe infection. The size of the growths is variable, but most are less than 1/8th inch (3 mm) in diameter. The surface of the growth is smooth and slightly irregular.

Treatment: There is no treatment for lymphocystis, and since the growths disappear in time, no treatment is recommended. However, if the growths interfere greatly with feeding or swimming, they can be removed at the risk of spreading the virus and causing secondary bacterial infection. Use a sterilized curved fingernail scissors or a convexly curved or straight toenail clippers to remove the growth at the base. Do this work while holding the fish above a treatment tank to prevent liberating viral material into the display tank. Antibiotic treatment is recommended to control bacterial infection.

METAZOAN PARASITES

There are numerous parasitic diseases of fish, internal and external, caused by large, relatively speaking, multicelled animals (metazoans) mostly in the categories of worms and crustaceans. Some of these have complicated life cycles involving intermediate hosts and can not reproduce in the aquarium, in which case they are only a threat to the infected fish. Others have simple life cycles and can, if given the chance, become a major problem. Fortunately, reproduction and growth is much slower than single celled parasites (protozoans) and infestations can be caught fairly early. Two of these larger parasites that occasionally show up in marine aquaria are discussed below and the recommended treatment for these can generally be applied to other metazoan parasites as well.

Fish Flukes

Benedenia melleni are flattened, almost transparent parasites that attach to the gills and external surfaces of fish. They are usually only about 1/8 inch long, but may reach a length of ½ inch. Their transparency makes them difficult to see and they are first noticed as numerous small bumps on the side of the fish. They may also infest the gills, but are usually evident on the body at the same time.

Symptoms: Fish that are infested actively scrape and swim against the bottom attempting to dislodge the parasites. Flukes can readily move from one fish to another, although they tend to remain with the same fish. Severe infestations invite bacterial infection by stressing and weakening the fish as well as by breaking through the skin and mucus layers.

Treatment: Benedenia can reproduce in the aquarium and although each generation takes several weeks instead of days, they can become epidemic. The best immediate treatment is a fresh water bath. Catch the fish as gently as possible to prevent the parasites from being dislodged and transfer the fish to a fresh water bath as described under the *Oodinium* section. The flukes will turn opaque and drop off the fish very quickly. The fish can be left in the bath, under careful observation, five to eight minutes if necessary if all the flukes do not drop off in two minutes. The fresh water bath can be repeated every day or so whenever the flukes are observed on fish and the flukes will soon be exterminated; which is fine if you can get fish out of the tank with very little effort. The traditional formalin bath, as described in the *Cryptocaryon* treatment section, is also effective against flukes and fish lice and can be used in conjunction with the fresh water bath.

 Another rather recently developed treatment for external worm and crustacean parasites is addition of the chemical o,o-dimethyl 2,2,2-trichloro-1-hydroxyethyl phosphonate directly to the tank water. For some strange reason, this chemical is usually referred to only as DTHP. It was developed as an insecticide and was found to be effective against many aquatic fish parasites. It has the advantages of not disturbing the activity of a biological filter, breaking down into harmless compounds within a few weeks, and is easily removed with activated carbon. Unfortunately, there is no way the average aquarist can test for the amount of DTHP present in tank water. A concentration of .75 to 1.0 mg per liter is an effective dose. This compound is very toxic to crustaceans and so all shrimp, crabs, lobsters and, to be on the safe side, all valuable invertebrates should be removed from the tank before treatment. It is compatible with copper medications. DTHP goes under the trade names of Dylox, Dipterex, and Proxol 80 as well as several others. Although DTHP is quite effective against flukes and fish lice and can be added directly to the tank, I recommend the traditional formalin treatment unless you have the laboratory expertise and equipment to calculate and prepare the proper dose for your tank.

Parasite pickers such as small French angelfish, neon gobies, and Pacific cleaner wrasse are helpful in controlling these large parasites. The slow reproduction rate of the parasite allows an active cleaner to defuse the population bomb.

Fish Lice

Argulus is one of a number of genera of marine crustaceans that are parasitic on fishes and go by the general name of fish lice. Their appearance is variable. *Argulus* have flat shield like bodies that help them grip the surface of the fish and the mouth parts are modified into a suction grip and sting. Most *Argulus*, however, are fresh water parasites. Some parasitic copepods partially embed themselves in the host fish with only the paired, elongated egg sacs noticably protruding. Others are not permanently attached to the host fish and can move from fish to fish feeding on skin tissues.

It is important to recognize the difference between a parasitic copepod problem and an occasional bloom of free living copepods. Parasitic copepods, especially epidemics of them, are rather rare in marine aquaria. On the other hand, a balanced aquarium with a solid functioning biological filter and good algal growth may frequently experience a bloom of free living tiny copepods. These tiny "bugs" are much smaller than parasitic "bugs" and swarm over the algae covered sides of the aquarium. Occasionally they move over the sides of fish and give rise to fears of parasites. Actually these tiny white copepods, less than a millimeter long, fit very well into the natural food chain of the aquarium. They feed on detritus and algal cells and are in turn fed upon by invertebrates and small fish. Their numbers can be controlled by more frequent filter cleanings, keeping algal growth under control, and by strong filtering action through a UV unit or a small pored mechanical filter. Control measures should be considered only if they are causing the fish obvious discomfort.

Symptoms: Scratching and scraping behavior of the fish indicates irritation from external parasites and careful observation will reveal the presence of fish lice or other parasite problems.

Treatment: Apply the same treatment as described for fish flukes. Embeded parasites may not respond to this treatment and if these are present, it is best to remove them individually with tweezers. Dab the point of removal with an antiseptic solution.

Old Age

Old age is not really one of the "dirty dozen". Fish, as all other animals, must die sometime, and if they bow out of old age in your aquarium, then you've done the best you can for them. A marine fish dying of old age in an aquarium used to be very unusual, so much so that it was seldom considered as a possible cause of death. Marine aquarology has now advanced to the point where keeping a fish one to five years is commonplace, and so, old age must now be considered when analyzing fish death. Many fish, for example neon gobies and jawfish, have only a one or two year life expectancy in the wild and others rarely exceed a five year life span. These fish often exceed their natural life span when kept under good conditions away from natural predators and disease. Marine fish, like all other animals, have immune systems that protect them from disease. The efficiency of this immune system declines with age, as do internal organs and musculature, and the fish become more susceptible to the onslaught of disease. So even if the death of an old fish can be blamed on a specific disease, old age may be the basic cause.

Symptoms: Old age often causes changes in the appearance of fish just as it does in other animals. Fins often get longer, teeth may become more prominent, colors may change and even the shape of the head and slope of the back may alter. Unlike mammals, fish never stop growing. The rate of growth slows considerably when fish reach maturity, but it never stops and fish continue to increase in size under normal environmental and nutritonal conditions. Thus, older fish tend to be the larger and heavier individuals. Considerable variation in growth rate, however, prevents use of size or weight as an accurate index of age.

Treatment: There is no treatment, of course, for old age. Just keep in mind that fish do grow old, sometimes quite rapidly, and this may make them more susceptible to common problems.

Please note: If you have to destroy and dispose of sick or dead fish, NEVER, NEVER release them in native waters. Although the chance that they will recover and establish a population of non-native fish or that a new disease will be introduced to plague native fish is rather remote, the possibility can not be risked. The best way to dispose of a dead fish is to put it in a plastic bag and send it out with the garbage.

TANK STERILIZATION

Sometimes, despite everything, it becomes necessary to "kill" a tank and begin all over again. This could happen because of severe neglect or an extremely persistent parasite or bacterial problem. Sterilization is almost like setting up a tank for the first time, and as far as the life forms in the aquarium are concerned, there is no difference. When the tank is sterilized, everything in the tank will be killed so be sure to remove all animals. Animals removed from the tank may be carrying the bug that caused the problem so they must be treated and quarantined for several weeks before putting them into other tanks. The agent for sterilization is chlorine, sodium or calcium hypochlorite, the active ingredient in liquid bleach and in the granular bactericidal chlorine used in swimming pools. You don't have to worry about using too much chlorine (within reasonable limits) to sterilize your tank, but there must be a high enough concentration to do the job.

The tank does not have to be dismantled to achieve sterilization. In fact, tearing the tank apart is a waste of time and effort unless the undergravel filter has been disrupted and must be repaired. The first thing to do is to remove all colored plastic ornaments, if there are any, as these may become discolored by the chlorine. Leave rocks and coral in place as these must be sterilized also. Especially in old aquariums, it is a good idea to remove

108

as much of the accumulated organic matter as possible before sterilization. The chlorine must oxidize all organics present and the less there is, the more thoroughly it can do its job. Also there is a tendency for foam to form when the chlorine breaks down the organics, and in extreme cases, it is possible for the foam to overflow the tank and cover half the living room. (Someone—wife, husband, mother or roommate, would never forgive you.) The easiest way to remove the organics is to scrape the sides and stir the bottom well, then siphon out all the accumulated debris and dirty water. Refill the tank with fresh water, this is cheaper than salt water and works just as well for this purpose. Put everything else that needs sterilization into the tank including hoses, tank covers (not lights) and cleaning tools. Chlorine is very hard on nets so it is best just to dip them well for a few minutes in the chlorine solution, rinse with fresh water and let them dry completely. Outside filters should be left operating but their contents must be discarded. Keep the air pump or power filter running and water circulating just as if the tank were in normal operation. Now add about one tablespoon of dry granular chlorine for each 20 gallons or a cup of liquid bleach for each 20 gallons. This dose should be enough to sterilize the entire tank. Stir the bottom filter again to eliminate any static areas and let the whole mess cook in its own juices for 12 to 24 hours. After this period, check to make sure that all algae has turned white, if not disintegrated, and that there are no brown or black areas left on the sides or in the filters. If everything is not absolutely white and clean, then add another dose of chlorine and wait another 12 to 24 hours. It would be unusual, though, if the first application did not do the job.

The thing to do next, under some circumstances, is to neutralize the chlorine. It isn't good to put too much chlorine into a septic tank and it won't do the lawn any good either. Add hypo (sodium thiosulphate) or a commercial dechlorinator until the chlorine is gone. You can test for this with an OTO swimming pool test kit or you can take a sample of the water, a cupful will do, and put in a few drops of food color. When the color of the food coloring doesn't change or bleach out, then there is very little, if any chlorine left in the water.

When the chlorine has been neutralized, the tank should be siphoned again and everything, including the gravel filter, rinsed with one or two changes of fresh water. After the tank has been cleaned and rinsed to your satisfaction, it can be refilled with salt water and the process of conditioning the filter with nitrifying bacteria can begin again.

As a brief summary, here is a list of treatment do's and treatment don'ts.

Treatment Do's

Do immediately remove dead and dying fish from aquaria.

Do isolate fish for treatment.

Do identify the problem before treatment.

Do change water in the treatment tank every two or three days.

Do keep the bottom of the treatment tank clean.

Do provide shelter for the fish in treatment.

Do keep light levels low in the treatment tank.

Do keep track of ammonia and nitrite levels if the treatment tank has a biological filter.

Do keep fish isolated until the cure is complete.

Do keep aquarium medications out of the reach of children!

Do use medications as directed.

Do monitor copper levels in treatment water every one or two days.

Do rinse any external filters with fresh water to prevent reinfection of a tank after treatment is complete.

Treatment Don'ts

Don't medicate unless necessary.

Don't continue to add copper without testing the current copper level.

Don't exceed .4 ppm copper. No more than .25 ppm copper for three weeks is all that should ever be necessary.

Don't use antibiotics in a tank with a biological filter.

Don't use an activated carbon filter with any type of medication unless the object is to quickly remove the medication from the water.

Don't use a UV filter with any type of medication.

Don't release live or dead fish in non-native waters!

Chapter 10

FOODS AND FEEDING
What, When and How

Feeding marine fish properly is just as essential to their health and well being as providing a good physical and chemical environment. In nature, fish are adapted physiologically and ecologically to certain types of food organisms. These specific foods provide the nutritional requirements of the fish within the adapted "life style" of that species. The same variations in feeding habits found in land animals also exist among fish. Some species, such as the grizzly bear, feed on a wide variety of organisms and others, like the Everglades kite that feeds only on the *Pomacea* (apple) snail, are very restricted in their diet. Whether broad or restricted, the natural diet provides the amount and balance of proteins, fats, carbohydrates, vitamins, and minerals that each species needs to maintain good health.

Fish with broad, unspecialized dietary requirements usually adjust easily to the foods and conditions of captivity, while fish with highly specialized diets may have difficulty. However, just because a fish feeds on only one type of organism in nature doesn't necessarily mean that that particular food organism must be available in the aquarium. A fish may be limited by its adaptive behavior patterns to certain food organisms, but still be capable of digesting and utilizing other foods. In other words, a wrasse specially adapted to feeding on certain crustaceans found deep within branching corals can meet its nutritional needs with other crustaceans, such as shrimp, or prepared fish foods when these are made available in the artificial aquarium environment.

There are two problems that must be overcome in feeding captive marine fish. The first is to get the fish to accept a substitute for the natural diet, and the second is to provide all the nutritional requirements in the substitute food. Fish that consume a wide variety of foods in nature are usually most adaptable to aquarium fare. This doesn't mean that it is impossible to keep fish with very limited natural diets such as some of the butterfly fish, but more care and effort must be used in the feeding program.

For maximum success with your fish, it is best to select species that are generalized feeders, columns 7 and 10 in Table 7, and feed a good variety of foods. Table 7 is intended as a general guide to the natural food preferences of each major group of fishes. There are some exceptions to these groupings (for example, a few species of snapper are plankton pickers rather than generalized bottom feeders), however, the table will give you an idea of the content and structure of the natural diet of most fishes. Each of the 11 natural food groups from Table 7 is listed below with comment to provide a better understanding of natural diets. A possible substitute for each category of natural food is also discussed.

Column 1, Algae and Seagrasses

The marine algaes are generally broken up into two artificial groups, microalgaes and macroalgaes. The microalgaes include all the small species that must be studied under a microscope. They include the one celled, free floating phytoplankton and the tiny filamentous and colonial growths that attach to solid substrates. The macroalgae, however, are large enough to be seen and examined without magnification and range from small thumbnail sized growths to kelp plants 40 feet or more in height. The seagrasses: turtle grass, eel grass and a few others, are true aquatic flowering plants that are not algaes at all. They often cover vast areas of shallow bottom in the vicinity of coral reefs. Fish, such as parrotfish and surgeonfish, that feed primarily on seagrasses and algaes are true herbivores, the browsers and grazers of the sea bottom. These fish can get along for a while on standard aquarium fare, but nutritional deficiencies (sunken stomach, loss of color, inactivity) eventually develop. Marine algaes are the best vegetable matter to add to the diet, but leafy vegetables such as spinach and lettuce can be substituted.

Column 2, Algaes

There are many, many species of macroalgaes that make up part of the diet of omnivorous fish. Some of these are injested incidentally as the fish feeds on small crabs, shrimp and mollusks and others are deliberately eaten. These algaes may make up 10 to 50 percent of the diet of many species, thus vegetable matter should be a basic part of their diet in captivity. Clownfish and batfish are good examples of fish that normally include a high percentage of algae in their diet.

113

Fish Type	Algae and seagrasses 1	Algaes 2	Algae and detritus 3	Sponges 4	Plankton pickers 5	Generalized bottom feeders 6	Fish feeders 7	Coral feeders 8	Crustacean feeders (primary) 9	Generalized invertebrates 10	Parasite pickers 11
Sharks						x					
Moray eels						xx	x				
Squirrelfishes									x		
Groupers						x					
Hamlets						x					
Grammas					xx					x	
Hawkfish					xx	x					
Cardinalfishes					x						
Sweepers					x						
Snappers						x					
Grunts						x					
Porgies										x	
Sea Chubs	x										
Mojarras										x	
Reef drums									xx	x	
Goatfishes										x	
Damselfishes			xx		xx					x	
Clownfishes		x			xx					x	
Wrasses						x				xx	x
Parrotfishes	xx							x			
Flounders						x					
Gobies			xx							x	x
Blennies			xx							x	
Jawfishes					x						
Scorpionfishes						x	xx				
Spadefish	x	x	x			xx					
Batfish		x				xx					
Butterflyfishes		x						xx		x	
Angelfishes		x		xx							x
Pompano									x		
Surgeonfishes, Tangs	x		x								
Triggerfishes	x									xx	
Filefishes	x							x		x	
Sea robins										x	
Trunkfishes		x		x						xx	
Boxfishes		x		x						x	
Puffers		x		x						xx	
Frog fishes							x				
Sea horses					x						
Pipefishes					x						
Dragonets			x							x	

TABLE 7. Principle food groups of the major types of fishes.

Two x's indicate the strongest preference.

114

Column 3, Algae and Detritus

Detritus is composed of a great variety of organic matter. Bits of algaes, organic flocculants, solid wastes from fish and invertebrates, coral slime, bacterial debris and small worms and crustaceans accumulate in sheltered nooks about the reef. This detritus and the small algaes and invertebrates associated with it make up a food source for many small fish. Species of gobies, blennies and damselfish are among those that utilize this resource. Detritus accumulates in well lighted aquariums and serves, among other things, to supplement the diet of species that normally feed on it. These species usually do well on normal aquarium foods in old, well established marine aquariums.

Column 4, Sponge

Sponges are about the simplest of the metazoans (many celled animals) and they exhibit many forms and colors. The typical bath sponge and vase sponge are only two of hundreds of types of sponges. A number of species grow in the reef environment and provide homes for many species of small fish and invertebrates. Sponges are incidentally ingested in small volume by most herbivorous fishes as they graze algae, but only adult angelfish consume sponges as the major dietary component. In fact, sponges compose 70 to 97 percent of the adult diet of Atlantic angelfish. Juvenile angelfish feed on small crustaceans and filamentous algaes. The diet of sponge feeders can not be easily provided in captivity, but fortunately the juveniles do well on a varied diet laced with vegetable matter, and adults and sub-adults can get by on the same foods.

Column 5, Plankton Pickers

Many small fish make all or part of their living by hovering in the water over the reef or burrow and feeding selectively on the planktonic organisms that continually wash over these areas with the currents. Zooplankters—primarily copepods, small shrimp, mysids, and many types of fish and invertebrate larvae—are the usual food items. The proteins of larval forms of fish, shrimp, crabs, etc. are essentially the same as the adults so these items make good food sources for plankton picking fish. Plankton may form only a part of the diet of some fish so it's important to also supply some plant food such as algae growths or leafy greens. Almost all larval fish feed on zooplankton, even if the adults are herbivores; so the planktonic pastures are really the foundation for all life in the sea. Plankton pickers in the aquarium do well on bits of shaved shrimp and fish, processed flake food, and other foods that drift about in the water before settling.

Column 6, Generalized Bottom Feeders

This category is composed mostly of large, non-specific carnivores, such as sharks, snappers and groupers, and includes many groups with juveniles important to the marine aquarist. These fish are opportunistic feeders although they may have a general preference for a specific group of food organisms. In nature, they feed on whatever foods are most abundant and available—vast schools of small fish, shrimp, juvenile lobster, swarms of polychaete worms, almost anything and everything during the season of its abundance. The flexibility of their food requirements make these fish easy to feed in captivity, although some species may have other physiological requirements that make them difficult to keep. Again, a varied diet with emphasis on bits of fresh frozen shrimp, clams, fish and other seafood will keep these fish healthy and happy until they outgrow the aquarium.

Column 7, Fish Feeders

Very few marine fish suitable for small home aquariums are totally piscivorous, a fancy name for fish eaters. Some of the scorpionfishes, notably the lionfishes, and the anglerfishes, frog fish and sargassum fish, come fairly close to being exclusively piscivorous. These fish can be trained to take other foods, but this requires time and patience. Slow moving piscivorous fish are usually so well camouflaged that they appear to be part of the reef. Small fish blunder near them, often attracted by fin modifications that look like small worms or algae growths, and are suddenly engulfed by the monstrous (to them) vacuum cleaner action of the scorpionfish's mouth. These fish are difficult to keep because of their preference for live food and their tendency to eat every other fish in the tank. They are best kept by themselves or with larger fish, and fed small freshwater fish. Guppies and bait minnows live quite long enough to get eaten when dropped into the lionfish's lair and fresh water fish do not carry parasites that can survive in marine waters. It is possible to train frog fish and lionfish to take dead minnows and even pieces of fish flesh by loosely attaching the food to a string or wire to give it motion.

Column 8, Coral Feeders

To feed on coral polyps, the soft animal hidden in the stony coral skelton, a fish must be able to either crush the hard coral or reach a tiny mouth into small protected areas to remove the animals therein. Both of these specialized modes of feeding can cause problems for the marine aquarist. Unless care and attention is taken in developing a diet for these fish, they will not be able to obtain proper nourishment. The tiny mouthed butterflyfish are the most difficult of this category to feed. Bits of shrimp and scallop or live *Tubifex* and white worms, *Enchytraeus albidus,* pressed into coral or irregular rock surfaces often stimulate these fish to begin feeding. This will also help the butterflyfish find food in a competitive aquarium situation, however, be sure that food presented in this manner does not go uneaten and foul the aquarium.

Column 9, Crustacean Feeders (primary)

These species feed primarily on small crustaceans, but are not above picking up a worm or clam or two from time to time. Small shrimps and crabs represent the major part of their diet so some crustacean flesh should be a staple part of their diet in captivity. If fish in nature feed almost exclusively on one type of organism, it is important to include that general type of food in their diet. Then you can be reasonably sure that all their required nutritional elements are available to them. Frozen shrimp is perhaps the easiest way to get crustacean material into your fish's diet.

Column 10, Generalized Invertebrates

Many, if not most, small tropical marine fish feed on a wide variety of small invertebrates with a little bit of algae included upon occasion. Although one group of organisms—shrimp, snails, clams, worms, crabs, etc.—may be most common in the diet of certain species, a broad variety of small invertebrates are represented. The organism of choice often changes as the fish gains in size and changes its habitat. Since the specific natural diets of most fish at different stages of development are relatively unknown, a variety of foods that includes some item from each basic group of invertebrates is most likely to provide all the basic nutritional needs.

Column 11, Parasite Pickers

A few popular marine aquarium fishes make part of their living, either as adults or during the juvenile stage, by removing external parasites from large fish. It is not unusual to watch a huge green moray eel wait patiently with open mouth while a neon goby flits about its head and mouth picking up food debris and small parasites. Large grouper often lean to one side against a coral head and allow small angelfish and gobies to move over its body and gills picking off external parasites. This cleaning behavior is quite fascinating and can readily be observed in a home aquarium if neon gobies are kept with larger fish. Obviously, one would not want to provide parasites as a food source in the tank; fortunately, parasite pickers do very well on a varied basic diet when parasites are not available.

AVAILABLE FOODS FOR MARINE TROPICAL FISH

There is a wide variety of foods available to marine aquarists, most at little cost, that will provide a good diet for almost all marine fish. Many of these foods are listed below, with comment, to help you develop the proper feeding program for your particular needs. There are three main categories listed: Prepared Diets, Plant Foods, and Animal Foods. The fish in a community tank should receive two small feedings of a prepared diet each day and one feeding from each of the other two categories once a day, or at least every other day to keep them in top condition. Most aquarists, however, can not put this much effort into a feeding regimen for their tank. Even though three or four relatively small feedings of varied foods per day is best, most marine fish can get by nicely on two feedings per day. A good dry flake food feeding in the morning and a feeding of natural animal and plant foods in the evening will keep most fish in good condition.

The following information may be more than you need or want to know about foods and feeding; and although you should be able to keep your marine fish healthy and happy with only a few of these options, it's good to know about a broad range of available foods and feeding techniques.

PREPARED DIETS

The prepared diet specially compounded for marine fish can be a great aid to the marine aquarist; however, total dependence on a prepared diet can cause nutritional problems. Convenience is the most obvious advantage of the prepared diet, but equally important are inclusion of protein variety plus a broad spectrum of trace nutrients including vitamins and minerals. Be careful of using diets compounded for fresh water fish, particularly trout and catfish, because these do not provide the proper nutritional balance for coral reef fishes. They can easily cause problems, such as fatty degeneration of the liver, if fed to excess. Prepared diets can be purchased already compounded, dry flake foods are the most popular form, or they can be made at home in a wide variety of mixtures. Four basic types of prepared diets are discussed below.

Dry Flake Foods

This is the most widely used, and abused, form of prepared diet. These are relatively inexpensive, considering the small

Figure 9. Commercial flake food for tropical fish can be ground into particles suitable for feeding to late larval and post larval marine fish. A mortar and pestle provides good control over the fineness of the grind.

amounts consumed by each fish and the convenience of feeding, and contain a wide variety of nutrients. The flake food you choose should be of high quality, 35 to 45 percent protein, and contain some plant material, hopefully including marine algaes and carotene. The flakes should be large and crisp and not small musty or moldy. Store the well sealed container in a dry, cool place (the refrigerator is a good place in a warm, damp climate), not next to a hot light fixture or near the spray of an air lift. Don't buy more than you can use in a month or two and make sure that the dealer's stock is fresh.

Remember that flake food is very dry and compressed, thus contains a lot of food energy in a small space. It's easy to habitually overfeed the stuff. Just think what it would be like to eat all your meals as a dry, highly compressed flake with only a glass of water to wash it down. Coral reef fish do not normally feed on the surface and when they do take floating food, they may also ingest air bubbles which can cause excessive buoyancy and disturb the digestive process. If this is a problem, soaking the food in a small volume of water before feeding eliminates floating food and surface feeding. Small fish, such as young clownfish, may gorge on dry food and develop a case of the "bloats" as the food expands in their stomach. When this happens, the abdomen of the fish is greatly distended and the fish continually fights to keep from floating at the surface. The cure for this condition is to stop feeding for a day and then feed mostly a wet food mix with only an occasional light feeding of dry food. Don't depend entirely on a dry flake food—fish need fresh plant and animal foods on a regular basis also.

The Seafood Paste Mix

There are many variations of a wet blended diet that you can mix up yourself, and if you have the time and interest, this is a good way to give your fish the best possible diet with the least amount of daily fuss. It will, however, take an hour or two to make up the food for one or two months of feeding—a relatively minor investment of time considering the aesthetic and monetary value of your marine display. Building your own diet for your fish also has the advantage of being able to adjust it for the type of fish you favor. Heavy on the greens for example, if you favor tangs and small angelfish.

Figure 10. The general purpose shrimp base food mix. Upper left, leafy green *Ulva* algae — Upper right, the red algae *Hypnea* — Lower left, small peeled shrimp — Lower right, frozen cubes of the blended food mix.

The basic ingredient to this mix is fresh frozen shrimp, scallops, clams, fish, lobster (if price is no object) or other crustacean. Animals that break down to a paste-like consistency when blended, such as shrimp, are preferred over those that become watery, like oysters. Clean the meat of all shell, scales or skin and blend it with a little water to a paste-like consistency. A blender or one of the new food processors works well for this task. Two or three types of seafood; shrimp, clams and fish are best if possible to provide a variety of nutrients. Other types of meat can also be added sparingly for additional variety. While this mixture is still in the blender (the average aquarist shouldn't need more than two or thre cups of prepared diet at any one time), add about 20 percent by volume of vegetable material. Unless marine algaes (*Caulerpa, Ulva, Hypnea,* etc.) are available, use a mixture of greens such as chopped spinach and lettuce. A spoonful or two of dry kelp powder can take the place of some vegetable matter.

Blend the vegetable material into the mixture quite well. A vitamin and mineral complex can be added at this time if desired. A single prenatal vitamin capsule or dose for expectant mothers is a good "shotgun" approach unless you want to do a little research and add the trace nutrients you feel would be best. Make up enough of the mixture to fill an ice cube tray, several cups, or as much as you will need for a month or two. The consistency can be controlled by adding water if its too dense and dry flake food if its too wet. The mixture is then frozen, either in ice cube trays or in spoonfuls on a wax paper tray. After the mixture is well frozen, the individual cubes can be stored together in a plastic bag in the freezer.

At feeding time, one of the cubes is removed and small pieces of the right size for your fish is snipped off and dropped into the aquarium. If the mix is the right consistency, it will hold together until consumed by the fish. It isn't good to just toss a chunk into the aquarium and forget it, for it can dissolve into the water if uneaten and add too much too quickly to the organic load of the aquarium. Those with many tanks may wish to use the following gelatine mix.

The Gelatine Mix

This diet is similar to the seafood paste mix, but is a little more versatile and a little more fuss to make. The ingredients can be quite varied because the whole thing is held together with gelatine instead of the protein paste of the fish or shrimp. The basic ingredients for the seafood mix can be used as the base for the gelatine mix. Many other ingredients such as trout pellets, kelp bits or powder and algae can be included either ground or whole. Use up to 10 or 15 percent by weight of unflavored animal gelatine and about 50 percent water to make the basic mix. Add a little less water if the basic ingredients are wet. It will probably take a few attempts before you settle on the best formula for your fish so don't be afraid to experiment if you decide to use the gelatine mix.

Dissolve the gelatine in the water at a temperature of 150 to 200 °F. Add the melted gelatine to the other ingredients when the temperature falls below 150 °F and stir until the mixture is smooth. Now add the vitamin and mineral supplements and, if you wish, a little green or red food coloring. The coloring aids the fish in seeing the food and helps the aquarist to find uneaten food so it can be removed before it decomposes. Pour the completed mix into a tray and chill until set. The mix can then be cut up into cubes and stored in a closed container in the refrigerator or freezer. Bite sized pieces should be cut or grated from the cube at feeding time.

The Plaster Mix

This mix has certain advantages, but may not be worth the bother of preparation to the average aquarist. "Plaster mix" you may be thinking, "has this guy developed a crack in his think tank?" But no, there is a good basis for a plaster mix. Most of the herbivorous fishes and some coral and sponge eaters spend a great deal of time biting and scraping at the reef to consume the proper amount of algae. Life is much easier in the aquarium and even if the fish get along on the change of diet, they miss the extensive feeding activity. In fact, in the absence of browsing activity, the dentition of some fish may grow long enough to cause feeding difficulties. The plaster mix allows these fish to feed under simulated natural conditions and gives them the exercise they need.

The basis of the plaster mix is simple, just prepare a small amount of a pure plaster of paris according to directions. Trace nutrients can be added while the mixture is still fluid as can food coloring if desired. Wet ingredients added to the plaster mix often interfere with hardening so the addition of the solid food ingredients must be carefully timed so that they can be folded in just before the plaster hardens. Adding them too soon may affect the hardening of the mix and adding them too late causes a rough, unblended mass. Chopped shrimp and fish, dry trout pellets, dry flake food with algae flakes, chopped spinach, and kelp or marine algaes are good inclusions. Make sure all excess water is removed from the ingredients before folding them into the hardening plaster. The food ingredients should only make up 10 to 15 percent of the total volume of the mix. Store unused mix in the refrigerator or freezer. Even though the food items are encased in plaster, they will still spoil readily so the uneaten food mix should be removed from the aquarium after four or five hours. This diet will be useful to the advanced aquarist who keeps large surgeonfishes and parrotfishes, although the average aquarist looking for a simulated natural feeding approach may also wish to experiment with the plaster mix diet.

ANIMAL FOODS: LIVE

Most coral reef fish consume animal food as a major portion of their diet, thus animal foods are most important to the marine aquarist. Fish, like most other wild animals, consume the entire live prey organism when feeding. This gives them access to minerals in hard parts and shells, plus vitamins from internal organs, and proteins and food energy in the flesh and fat. Obviously, a variety of live food organisms is the best possible diet for most fish, and equally obviously, only a most unusual marine aquarist can supply their fish with an exclusive diet of varied live foods. However, there are a number of live foods that can be provided.

Brine Shrimp

Brine shrimp are the most common live food marine aquarists offer their fish. They are generally available in small portions as live adults or as dry eggs (cysts) that the aquarist

Figure 11. Brine shrimp eggs (cysts). The dried eggs of brine shrimp can be purchased in large cans or in small vials. Once the container is opened the eggs should be tightly sealed and stored in the refrigerator. It is wise to purchase no more than you can use up in a few months.

124

hatches as necessary. Opinions on the value of live, adult brine shrimp differ greatly among marine aquarists. Although live, clean and well fed adult brine shrimp are generally conceded to be an attractive and nutritious food (but not as an only food) for most marine tropicals, some aquarists fear introduction of bacteria and parasites from unclean cultures of brine shrimp. Adult brine shrimp can also be obtained in frozen and freeze dried forms. Frozen brine shrimp can lose much of their nutritive value (58% protein) if they are not handled properly. Thawing and refreezing, or slow initial freezing, causes ice crystals to form in the tissues. Ice crystals rupture cells and internal organs and cause most of the fluids to leave the shrimp before feeding. Thus the nutritional value of thawed and refrozen brine shrimp is limited to the protein in the exoskeleton.

Adding frozen brine shrimp directly to the tank as a small block and allowing the fish to snap them up as they drift off the block provides the most complete shrimp possible for the fish. However, it also allows all juices and materials frozen in the shrimp block to escape into the tank. Thawing the block in water and straining the shrimp from the accompanying liquid eliminates adding unnecessary organics to the tank, but it may also eliminate much of the food value of the brine shrimp. If the brine shrimp were quick frozen live in clean water, it's best to just drop a small block in the tank and let the fish go to it. However, if the shrimp were frozen after they were dead for awhile, or frozen too slowly, or thawed and refrozen one or more times; it's probably best not to feed them to the fish at all. Thaw a small part of the block in a clear glass and observe the result. If the water turns brown and the shrimp are nothing more than empty shells, it's a good bet the fish will gain little from eating them.

Freeze dried brine shrimp have a strong tendency to float since they have no water at all in their tissues. It is best to soak these shrimp in fresh water so that they sink and drift in the currents when introduced into the aquarium. Ingestion of a large amount of dry food can cause difficulties for marine fish.

Newly hatched baby brine shrimp (napulii) can be very valuable to the marine aquarist. They are easy to hatch and can be used to feed small plankton feeding fish such as damselfish and jawfish, many filter feeding invertebrates, and young fish of many species. Brine shrimp are very small when they hatch, not much bigger than a comma on a printed page, but even so, you may be amazed at the large size of many fish that eagerly eat them.

Hatching is quite simple. All that is necessary is a gallon jar of full salinity sea water or artificial salt mix (even a straight rock salt mix will do) and an air stone for aeration. Bubble the salt water and brine shrimp egg mixture vigorously so that the eggs do not accumulate at the surface. The jar should be filled about 3/4ths full to reduce spray from the bottle. A cap with a hole for the air tubing or a plug of cotton also reduces spray from the hatching jar. A jug with a narrow neck is good, but it can't be cleaned as easily as a wide mouth jar. One or two teaspoons of eggs should provide plenty of hatchlings for most aquarists. The eggs hatch within 24 hours at temperatures of about 80°F. At temperatures in the low 70's, hatching may take up to 48 hours. Time of hatching and yield of brine shrimp depends greatly on egg quality and the set up of the hatching jar. Keep temperatures above 75°F and allow light, preferably sunlight, to reach the hatching jar.

Figure 12. Two inexpensive, effective brine shrimp hatcheries. The average aquarist and small breeder will seldom need more of a hatchery than one or two gallon jugs and an air supply. The floss plug in the top of the jug allows air to escape but keeps eggs and spray inside. A larger hatching jar can be made by cutting the bottom off a five gallon plastic water jug and supporting it in a wooden frame or even in a large bucket. Although an inverted cone or pyramid shape makes a more efficient hatchery, the above devices will work well for the home aquarist.

For about eight hours after hatching, baby brine shrimp sink to the bottom and empty egg shells float at the surface when aeration is removed. A very clean separation can be obtained from good quality eggs at this time. It is an easy matter to insert a small siphon into the jar and draw off the hatchlings from the bottom of the jar. Be sure to wait 15 or 20 minutes to let the shells and the hatchlings separate and break the siphon before the floating egg shell reach the bottom of the jar. Newly hatched brine shrimp are strongly attracted to light and can be concentrated at one spot by a narrow beam of light. If the hatch goes too long before separation, two or three days, the hatchlings remain mixed with the egg shells at the surface and separation is difficult. If this occurs, the best method of separation is to use light to concentrate the hatchlings away from the empty shells. An elaborate separation box can be constructed that allows the new hatch to swim from a dark compartment to a lighted compartment under a partial partition that prevents the floating eggs from leaving the darkened compartment. A simpler procedure, but less effective, is to shield the hatching jar with a piece of black paper that has a hole about an inch in diameter, position the hole a few inches above the bottom of the jar and shine a light on the hole. The light will draw the baby brine shrimp from the surface and cluster them about the light. They can be easily siphoned from the jar after they have had time to gather about the lighted area.

A fine mesh net can be used to separate the hatchlings from the culture water and concentrate them in a small volume for feeding to the fish or invertebrates. Baby brine shrimp have a dense oily yolk sac that gives them an orange or yellow color. It is possible to over feed young fish on new hatched brine shrimp and cause fatty degeneration of the liver. Thus, feed baby shrimp carefully to young fish and be sure that they do not over feed on this very attractive food.

Brine shrimp eggs are properly termed cysts and they have gone through the early stages of development while still attached to the mother. These cysts (eggs) drop off the female and drift to the shore of the brine shrimp ponds where, in most species, they must undergo a dry period before complete development and hatching can occur. It is after they are deposited in wind rows along the shore that they are collected, processed and packaged. The dry eggs are separated from debris and bad eggs by first sieving to recover all eggs and then air blowing to remove the lighter, unhatchable eggs. The heavier, good eggs can be kept viable for many years when sealed in a vacuum pack.

Live Fish

A number of popular marine aquarium fish: lion fish, panther fish, groupers and small snappers, sargassumfish and angler fish, either require or enjoy small live fish in their diet. It is best to feed small fresh water fish because they are less expensive than marine fish, and most important, do not carry marine diseases and parasites. Goldfish, guppies and mollies serve this purpose well and stay alive long enough in the marine tank to entice the predator to strike. Some aquarists who keep piscivorous fishes maintain breeding colonies of guppies or mollies as fodder fish for their marine predators. If you do feed small fish from a marine or brackish water source, be sure to give them a two minute fresh water bath before feeding to remove external parasites.

Small Shrimp and Other Crustaceans

An occasional feeding of live food is one of the best things you can do for the diet of your marine fish. Small live crustaceans are not too difficult to find if you are willing to spend a little time and effort. A fine mesh dip net or seine worked in grass beds in fresh or marine areas will often provide a surprising number of small shrimp, amphipods, crabs, worms, etc. and most of these are excellent live food organisms for your marines. Give the marine organisms a quick dip in fresh water to reduce the possibilities of parasite introduction. The fresh water dip (salt water dip for fresh water organisms) is a good way to either kill or incapacitate the organisms so that the fish can snap them up before they find shelter in the bottom of the tank. You may be surprised at how much small crustacean life already exists in your marine tank. Fish usually feed only in the day time and many small crustaceans are active only at night. Old well established tanks often develop a population of amphipods that can only be observed crawling about algae covered rocks and walls several hours after dark. Examination of the tank by flashlight at some time well into the night may reveal aspects of your aquarium you never knew existed.

Rose Coral

Rose coral is a solitary coral found near coral reefs in tropical seas. The common species in Florida waters is *Manicina areolata*. Because it is a solitary coral, rose coral is easily collected, handled, and shipped and most coral polyp eating fish enjoy an occasional treat of fresh coral. Coral does not live long in captivity under the normal aquarium conditions so be sure it is alive and in good condition before purchase. The flesh embedded in the coral skeleton should be firm and brown or greenish in color. It should not smell putrid or of decomposition when removed from the water and held to the nose. This coral can be frozen and kept fresh for long periods, however it will quickly decompose when fed after being frozen, so do not add more than the fish will eat within a few hours if the coral is not alive.

Tubifex Worms

Tubifex worms have always been popular with fresh water aquarists, but they also have an application in marine aquariums as well. One very useful method of feeding *Tubifex* worms is to press a small ball of worms deeply into a coral skeleton and then place it in the tank. Hard to feed fish such as butterfly fish are often attracted by the movement of the worms and begin to feed actively. Use caution when feeding *Tubifex* worms. They can quickly foul a tank if overfed to marine fish. Be sure to wash the ball of worms very well before feeding and remove all dead worms and decaying organic matter. *Tubifex* worms, like the organisms mentioned below, should not be a major portion of the diet.

Other Possibilities

Some marine aquarists with a background in freshwater fish keeping may wish to experiment with other typical live freshwater fish foods such as whiteworms, *Enchytraeus albidus,* earth worms and fruit fly larvae. These are good occasional foods and may have some special uses for certain fish, but remember that the proteins and fats are not those that marine fish digestive systems have evolved to handle. A diet rich in these foods may cause liver problems for marine fish. Make sure that these foods are cleaned before introducing them to the tank. Wash worms and fly larvae carefully and try to remove all dead organisms before feeding the live ones. Earth worms are a good food, but the intestines carry much soil (the earthworms natural food) and this soil must be removed before the worm is cut up and fed. Strip this soil from the worm by squeezing the worm between the thumb and index finger and pull the worm between the fingers to eject the contents of the digestive tract.

ANIMAL FOODS: DEAD

Most marine aquarists can not feed live foods to their fish on a regular basis, and fortunately, most fish do well on foods that can be stored in the freezer or on the shelf.

Shrimp

Shrimp is one of the best basic foods for marine fish. Crustaceans of one type or another are a major part of the diet of many marine fish, and shrimp, being a common marine crustacean, is a good substitute for the natural diet. Shrimp can be obtained in frozen packages designed as tropical fish food or as shrimp from the market in either fresh or frozen form, which is also excellent for marine fish. There are numerous methods for feeding shrimp to marine fish. In almost all instances the shrimp should be peeled and washed to remove the hard exoskeleton and excess fluids. Perhaps the easiest method of handling this basic food is to freeze the washed shrimp into a fist sized ball and keep it in a plastic bag in the freezer. Select a metal grater that shaves particles of the proper size for the fish to consume in one bite. More than one size grater can be used if small and large fish are kept together. The proper portion can be grated from the ball at each feeding time. Thus one preparation of shrimp can last for several weeks and feeding is quick and simple. It is also possible to grate the entire portion of frozen, peeled shrimp at one time either with the grater wheel of a food processor or with a bit of elbow grease on a manual model. The shrimp bits can then be frozen in portions packed for each feeding, and then feeding for the next few weeks consists only of dropping the premeasured frozen cubes of shrimp bits into the tank.

Mollusks

After Crustaceans, mollusks are one of the most common food items in marine fish diets. Scallops, squid, clams, oysters and conch are the most commonly encountered in food, bait and fish food products. All of the above can be utilized by the marine aquarist in the same manner as shrimp. Most mollusks are not as gelatinous as shrimp and although they are readily grated into small pieces when frozen, the pasty, binding quality of shrimp is absent. Alternate one or more of the mollusks with shrimp or mix them together to provide a good mix of animal protein.

Processed Plankton

Marine plankton is now available as frozen, dried, and freeze dried products. This plankton comes from the nutrient rich cold waters of the Arctic and Sub Arctic regions of the Atlantic and Pacific oceans. It is composed primarily of small euphasid shrimp and/or calanoid copepods and is rich in protein (60 to 70 percent), wax esters and lipids. Cold water, northern plankton is not a natural food of marine tropicals; however, it is a good, but rich, fish food and one should be careful not to overfeed, especially with the dry form of the product. Plankton feeding should enhance the condition and color of your marines.

Fish

Ocean fish is another good source of animal protein for your marines. Most small reef fish do not commonly eat fish as they are not equipped to chase and capture them. However, when an injured or dead fish presents the opportunity, most are quick to partake of their hapless comrade. Boneless fish flesh can be prepared and fed similar to peeled shrimp. Be careful not to overfeed because fish seems to have a greater tendency to foul the aquarium water than shrimp or scallop. All fish products, like all marine animal foods, should be hard frozen before feeding to reduce the possibility of parasite introduction. Fish roe and fish liver are also excellent foods for marines. These foods are best fed by snipping small pieces off a frozen block and feeding them slowly. Fish roe has much oil and shouldn't be fed to excess, but a little bit now and then will provide many of the nutrients that may be missing or altered in other foods. Watch the color of your fish improve after feeding fish roe once or twice a week.

Other Meats

Lean beef, beef liver, and beef heart are often recommended for feeding to marines and fresh water fish. An occasional feeding of these products is helpful if seafoods just aren't available and the only alternative is a constant dry food diet. If you must feed meat of land animals, rabbit and chicken may be better because there is less fat in their flesh. Remember that fish are cold blooded (poikilothermic) and all digestion reactions take place at 70 to 80 °F, the temperature of the aquarium water, thus, they may not efficiently digest the types of fats present in the flesh of warm blooded animals. They are much better off with the flesh of animals that are similar to their normal prey.

PLANT FOODS

As mentioned previously, vegetable matter is an important part of the diet of most marine fish. Tropical marine algaes, since they are the natural plant foods, are much desired for inclusion in the diet. Broad, thin, green algaes such as *Caulerpa* and *Ulva* and meaty red and browns such as *Hypnea, Gelidium* and *Dictyota* are commonly found in stomach contents analyses, and are best for feeding. These algaes can be added to prepared diets or washed with fresh water and placed in the aquarium as browse for the fish. Unfortunately, most marine aquarists do not have ready access to tropical marine algaes and one must also be able to identify the desirable types among hundreds of species of unsuitable calcareous and filamentous species.

Substitutes for tropical marine algaes are available. Pacific kelp is used as a human food supplement and is available in health food and grocery stores, usually in dried form. Greens can be supplied by inclusion of chopped spinach and/or turnip greens and an occasional leaf of lettuce. These can be included in the prepared diet or fed as browse in the aquarium. Be sure to remove uneaten greens after a day or two to prevent them from rotting in the tank.

FEEDING INVERTEBRATES

Most active invertebrates: shrimp, lobsters, and crabs prefer a chunk of solid food that they can hold and tear apart with their mouth parts. These animals often feed at night and are adept at finding small food particles that the fish may have lost during the day. A few small pieces of frozen shrimp or fish dropped into the tank after lights out will usually keep these animals well fed since they don't have to compete with the fish after dark.

Good algae growth in the tank keeps most of the slow moving grazers like nudibranchs and sea urchins quite happy. If you live near the sea, a rock heavy with marine growth provides much food for invertebrates and some fish. However, beware of parasite introduction. Unless the "live rock" is put through a quarantine, it may be best to restrict it to an "invertebrate only" tank.

Many of the invertebrates now kept are basically plankton feeders: tube worms, some anemones, corals and bivalve mollusks. They all have some sort of feeding mechanism that catches or filters out the tiny planktonic organisms that normally surround them. There are two ways to feed these animals with live organisms—introducing the food organisms to the tank and removing the invertebrate from the display tank to place it in a feeding tank. Newly hatched baby brine shrimp are a very good food because they are nutritious, do not foul the aquarium, are easy to produce, and are readily taken by filter feeders. Wild caught live ocean plankton is also very good, but besides being difficult to get, it may also introduce disease organisms.

A baster is a handy tool at feeding time. Concentrate the brine shrimp in a cupful or two of salt water and use the baster to direct a stream of brine shrimp napulii into the vicinity of the invertebrates. Some animals such as small anemones that are attached to a moveable rock, feather duster worms and barnacles can be removed from the aquarium and placed in a bucket or small tank with a high concentration of new hatch brine shrimp and good aeration. After several hours they will be well fed and can be replaced in the display tank.

Anemones

Anemones are beautiful animals, but difficult to keep. They require the highest quality water and intense, full spectrum lighting to keep them in good condition. Anemones of the genera *Stoichactis* and *Radianthus,* typical clownfish anemones, trap and feed on larger invertebrates and fishes as well as planktonic creatures in nature, thus they relish a piece of shrimp or fish once or twice a week. If a clownfish is kept with the anemone, it can often be persuaded to feed its companion by giving the clownfish a morsel of food too big for the fish to swallow. The clown usually carries the food to the anemone and obligingly thrusts it deeply into the tentacles. Fine tentacled anemones also take small planktonic food so it is good to give them an occasional feeding of live baby brine shrimp. Anemones, like their cousins the corals, also obtain nourishment a third way. Their tissues contain living algal cells called *Zooxanthellae;* and in exchange for a protected place to live, these algal cells produce food by photosynthesis in excess of their needs and supply the anemone with this additional food energy. Lighting must be intense and close to full spectrum to provide the algal cells buried in the anemone's tissues with enough light for photosynthesis. This is why anemones in captivity so often fade to whiteness and gradually wither away to nothing and die. Once the anemone has turned completely white or cream colored, all the algal cells are gone and the anemone is on a downhill ride that is almost impossible to reverse. It may live another six months or so, but will lose condition, get very much smaller and eventually die. The only remedy is to insure adequate light while the anemone is still in good condition. A few hours of sunlight every day is very helpful and should be arranged if at all possible. An incandescent bulb, 60 watts or better, can be put in a reflector and placed outside the tank very near the anemone to supplement the normal tank lighting, which should be 40 to 80 watts of full spectrum florescent lighting. The incandescent bulb will provide the right spectrum and increase the total light the anemone receives, but it will also increase the temperature of the aquarium and this effect must be carefully controlled. The incandescent light can be put on a timer to cycle the light for an exposure time that will not greatly increase the tank temperature.

Chapter 11

BREEDING MARINE FISH
The Basic Process

Not very long ago, as late as the early 70's, it was possible to find authoritative quotes in the aquarium literature stating that marine tropical fish could not be successfully reared in commercial numbers because the particular conditions required by the delicate larvae could not be consistently maintained. This was certainly true up to the late 60's, but at that time increased interest and experimentation in propagation of marine food fish stimulated development of new techniques that could be transferred, with some modifications, to the culture of some marine tropical fish. Propagation of pompano, the gourmet's fish of our subtropical waters, was the subject of intense and highly competitive effort by several commercial firms and government laboratories. These efforts, some biologically successful and some not, have all been dropped or redirected due to financial, economic and technical difficulties; however some individuals involved in these projects have shifted their knowledge and talents to propagation of marine tropicals. Although developing slowly, farming of marine tropical fish has a strong toehold and should continue to expand.

It was soon apparent that the most immediate financial rewards lay not with food fish culture, although the market was vast (as was the capital requirements), but in propagation of marine tropical fish. For even though the market was far smaller than food fish, the price per unit was far higher. Thus, in late 1972 and early 1973 I began to work at home in my garage on the problems of rearing marine tropical fish, and succeeded in early 1973 in rearing thousands of juvenile "percula" or common clownfish, *Amphiprion ocellaris,* from two spawning pairs. The early part of this work was reported in the March-April 1973 issue of *Salt Water Aquarium Magazine,* Vol. 9, No. 2, published by the late Robert P.L. Straughan. Mr. Straughan contributed greatly to the development of the marine aquarium hobby and was always optimistic about the possibilities of rearing marine tropicals in large numbers. It seemed appropriate that the first account of rearing large numbers of a marine tropical fish should

Figure 13. The "Hijack". A unique fish made possible only by controlled marine fish culture. The mother was a high-hat, *Equetus acuminatus*, and the father was a jackknife fish, *Equetus lanceolatus*. This man made hybrid does not exist in nature.

appear in his publication. Since that time there has been much activity and many published articles dealing with marine tropical fish propagation; and many species have been reared through the larval stage, although only a few in commercial numbers. Aqualife Research first marketed tank reared clownfish and neon gobies in 1973 and since then, several other companies have begun rearing clownfish. Thus, because of the increased activity, there should be a good selection of tank reared marine tropicals on the market in future years. The basic technology is here, but in most instances, additional time and effort is required to bring these species into commercial production.

The species of marine tropical fish that have been spawned and reared to the juvenile stage include, but are not restricted to, the listing in table 8.

Common name	Scientific name
Skunk clownfish	*Amphiprion akallopisos*
Orange-fin clownfish	*A. chrysopterus*
Clarkii clownfish	*A. clarkii*
Red saddle clownfish	*A. ephippium*
Tomato clownfish	*A. frenatus*
Cinnamon clownfish	*A. melanopus*
Percula (common) clownfish	*A. ocellaris*
Percula clownfish	*A. percula*
Pink skunk clownfish	*A. perideraion*
Saddleback clownfish	*A. polymnus*
Australian clownfish	*A. rubrocinctus*
Orange skunk clownfish	*A. sandaracinos*
Three-band clownfish	*A. tricinctus*
Maroon clownfish	*Premnas biaculeatus*
Royal gramma	*Gramma loreto*
Cardinalfish	*Apogon* sp.
Florida pompano	*Trachinotus carolinus*
Grey snapper	*Lutjanus griseus*
Porkfish	*Anisotremus virginicus*
White grunt	*Haemulon plumieri*
High-hat	*Equetus acuminatus*
Jackknife-fish	*E. lanceolatus*
Atlantic spadefish	*Chaetodipterus faber*
Grey angelfish	*Pomacanthus arcuatus*
French angelfish	*P. paru*
Sargeant major	*Abudefduf saxatilis*
Garibaldi	*Hypsypops rubicundus*
Yellowtail damselfish (Jewelfish)	*Microspathodon chrysurus*
Hogfish	*Lachnolaimus maximus*
Yellowhead jawfish	*Opistognathus aurifrons*
Greenband goby	*Gobiosoma multifasciatum*
Sharknosed goby	*G. evelynae*
Neon goby	*G. oceanops*
Skilletfish	*Gobiesox strumosus*
Lined seahorse	*Hippocampus erectus*
Dwarf seahorse	*H. zosterae*
Northern puffer	*Sphoeroides maculatus*

TABLE 8. Marine fishes reared from laboratory hatched spawns.

There are reports of other species being reared and I have probably missed a few, but these are the marine "tropicals" that I am sure have been reared into the juvenile stage. There are many other species that have been spawned and reared for only a few days into the larval stage and many others that have been reared from wild spawned eggs taken in plankton tows. Also some food and bait species of tropical and subtropical waters not mentioned here have also been reared very successfully. Thus, the basic technology exists to rear many important marine aquarium fishes, and tank reared fish may become a significant part of the future of the marine aquarium hobby.

Propagation of marine tropical fish has progressed slowly for many reasons; but perhaps the most important of these is the lack of understanding, and the difficulties of creating, the pelagic environment essential for larval survival. Since wide spread marine aquarium keeping is a relatively recent development, the basic concepts of aquatic life held by most aquarists relate to fresh water experience. Fresh water fish reproduction usually involves some processes we can readily understand and that fit in well with our preconceived ideas of terrestrial animal reproduction. Things such as nest making, live birth, baby fish that can be easily seen with the naked eye, baby fish that swim in schools, parental care of eggs and parental protection of baby fish, and all of the above taking place in a bottom type environment are all basically familiar. It is natural to retain these concepts when we move from fresh water to marine aquariums. Unfortunately, these fresh water concepts about the nature of the watery world can cause a number of misconceptions about what we see in the marine environment. Marine fish do not care for their young once they have hatched. In fact, since most marine fish spend their larval period as a part of the plankton, plankton feeding fish quickly eat their own young if they happen to drift by. During their time in the plankton, larval fish are totally dependent on planktonic microorganisms for food, and although they can move about within the space of a few feet at most, major movement is dependent on ocean currents during their early larval life.

Reproduction of marine fish can be categorized in four basic patterns. The most common is release of tiny, transparent, free floating eggs with complete absence of parental care. Angelfish, butterflyfish, tangs, groupers, snappers, wrasses, grunts, drums, and parrotfishes are among those with this type of reproductive

138

Figure 14. The pelagic egg of the French angelfish. The egg, bounded by the large circle in the center of the photomicrograph, has a diameter of about one millimeter, the thickness of a dime. The two center circles are the first two cells of the developing embryo. They appear about 30 minutes after fertilization and are located at the bottom of the floating egg. The indistinct dark circle in the center of the egg is an oil droplet located at the top that provides the buoyancy to keep the egg floating near the surface.

Figure 15. The pelagic prolarva of the French angelfish at the moment of hatching. Hatching occurs about 20 hours after fertilization. The hatchling is in the prolarval stage, little more than a yolk sac and tail when it breaks out of the flexible egg shell. Two full days must pass before fins, eyes, and gut are developed well enough for the larva to begin to feed.

139

style. The second most common mode is attachment of the eggs to a bottom substrate as a type of nesting behavior. These are termed demersal eggs, in contrast to the free floating pelagic eggs, and the resulting larvae may be large as with clownfish or quite small as with damselfish. Gobies, blennies, damselfish and clownfish are the common nest building marines. A variation on the demersal theme is oral incubation of eggs or mouth brooding. Instead of attaching the eggs to the bottom, the male retains them in his oral cavity during the period of incubation. Jawfish and cardinalfish are mouth brooders. A very few marine species, such as sea horses, give birth to well developed live young.

Mouth brooders and those fish that lay demersal eggs produce far fewer eggs than fish that spawn pelagic eggs. These species aerate and protect their eggs from predators during early development, thus attain an economy of reproductive energy in exchange for a period of parental care. Nesting and mouth brooding species incubate their eggs from three to ten days depending on the species and the young are hatched with a small residual yolk sac, fully developed eyes and mouth parts, and the ability to swim with purpose and direction. Their early larval period is passed as a creature of the plankton, but the helpless egg and pro-larval stage of a pelagic egg is avoided and the total larval period is usually shortened. The spawn of species that protect their eggs varies in number from a low of 50 to 100 to a high of 10 to 15 thousand, whereas those species that spawn pelagic eggs can produce well over 200 thousand eggs or more per spawn and may spawn on almost a daily basis during the height of the spawning season. Of course small species such as pigmy angelfish spawn fewer eggs, only 300 to 500 per spawn, but these spawns can also occur on a daily basis. The larvae that hatch from pelagic eggs are completely helpless. They carry a large yolk sac and have not yet formed pigmented eyes, a functional gut or mouth parts, and the paired fins are still mere buds. Another 72 hours must pass before these larvae develop to the point that the yolk sac is consumed and they can swim and feed on their own.

The popular aquarium literature in recent years has hosted numerous articles on rearing marine tropical fish, and most of these were of some help to aspiring culturists. However, successful rearing of marine fish requires consistent care, detailed observation, some basic knowledge, and a good bit of experience. The printed page can not supply the dedication and actual experience, but it can give the basic information and some suggestions on technique along with the knowledge that it can be done. In this chapter, I will try to summarize the information already available on rearing clownfish in the light of my own experience and present a guide to the basics of rearing clownfish. Clownfish are among the easiest of all marine tropicals to rear and this information is specifically directed towards them since they give the amateur marine fish breeder the best chance to succeed. There are a number of other species that the amateur marine breeder may be able to rear as the quintessence of the marine fish keeping experience. These are: neon gobies and other species of gobies and blennies, sea horses, royal grammas, jawfish and other species of clownfish. These fish, except sea horses, are more difficult than clownfish, but are definite future possibilities for the amateur marine breeder.

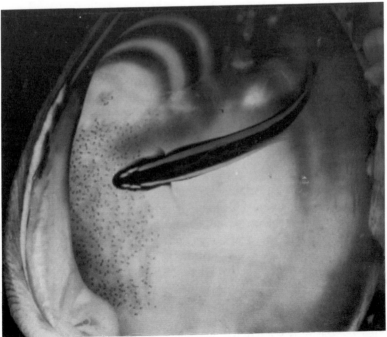

Figure 16. The male neon goby, *Gobiosoma oceanops*, guarding his nest under a clam shell. The male takes on the task of keeping the eggs tended in the secret nest. The eggs are near hatching and the well developed eyes of the embryos can be seen through the transparent eggs.

SPAWNING

Marine tropical fish are not unlike all other creatures of the earth that depend on sexual reproduction to continue their species. The drive to reproduce is extremely strong, and they *will* spawn, providing, and this is a crucial providing, that the environment and the physical condition of the fish meet the species' minimum requirements for reproduction. The problem, therefore, is to identify and provide the necessary conditions for each species that is to be spawned. The four basic criteria are:

1. Adult fish in good health.
2. Proper nutrition—quality and quantity.
3. Suitable physical environment—light, temperature and surroundings.
4. Proper chemical environment—water quality.

Obviously, all the proper conditions exist in nature during the spawning season so we must look to the wild to find clues to the conditions that must be created. The following discussion is directed toward the common or percula clownfish, *Amphiprion ocellaris,* but can apply in principle to other species.

The fish must be adult, that is of the proper size and age for spawning activity, and must be in good physical condition. There must be male and female fish present, in the case of clownfish one of each sex is all that is necessary. In fact, unless the aquarium is quite large, a mated pair will seldom allow others of their species to survive within the tank. Other species, however, such as wrasses and damsels, may need to aggregate in small groups before spawning behavior is stimulated. I have found no sure color markings on percula clownfish that differentiate male and female, but there are size and shape differences between adults. The female is larger and more robust than the male, and when the gonads are active, the abdomen is quite rotund. The adult male is perhaps half to three quarters the size of the full grown female and is slim without the heavy belly of the female. Given a population of adult fish, these size and and shape characteristics are sufficient to select sexes with about 90% accuracy. Immature fish and young adults can not be accurately sexed on appearance—indeed they are probably all potential males at an early age.

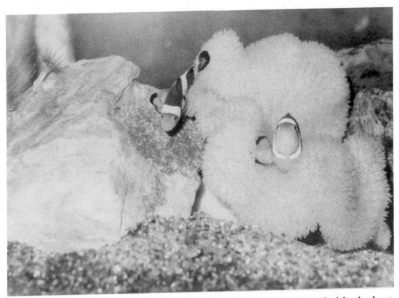

Figure 17. The common clownfish, *Amphiprion ocellaris*, is probably the best known of the demersal spawning marine tropical fish. The nest is usually laid at the base of an anemone and the male does most of the babysitting.

Sex reversal has recently been demonstrated in seven species of clownfish. The sex change is protanderous, from male to female, and is apparently stimulated by changes in the social structure of the group. In the wild, one dominant female, an adult male, and a variable group of subadult fish inhabitat the same general area about a host anemone. The smaller fish are repressed in sexual development by the presence of the active pair. They do not mature sexually or grow in size. If the adult male is lost to a predator, the largest of the subadult fish rapidly matures into a male and becomes the female's mate. If the female is lost, the active male changes relatively quickly into a female and mates with the now maturing new male. Nature thus assures that every host anemone will have a functional pair of clownfish without regard to any predetermined genetic sex distinction.

Since it is often difficult to find adult fish in good condition, it is usually best to grow your own clownfish brood stock. It takes a little patience, 6 to 18 months depending on their size when you begin, but there is the advantage of often winding up with more than one pair. Start with a good established tank of at least 20 gallons, 40 is better, and then purchase 8 to 12 healthy young clownfish. Statistically, you need a minimum of 6 fish to assure that at least one of each sex is present, assuming an equal distribution of sexes and no artificial selection in choice of fish. Statistics also do not allow for sex change, but this phenomenon works to the advantage of the aquarist in the case of clownfish, unless one begins with sexually mature fish.

If you begin with juvenile fish, tank reared clowns are good for the initial breeding stock since they haven't been exposed to treatment or collection chemicals, but wild caught fish should do just as well if they are in good condition. Depending on their age and size, the fish will coexist peacefully for awhile until they begin to pair. An anemone, preferably a pacific carpet anemone, will promote natural behavior patterns, thus be an aid to pairing and spawning. When a pair forms, the two fish become protective of a territory about the anemone and prevent any other fish of the same or closely related species from entering their area. The territorial imperative is so intense that a strong pair will destroy the hapless fish that can not flee their boundaries. The new pair, or the other fish, must be removed soon after agressiveness is first displayed to prevent loss of the unpaired fish. Other pairs may also form from the unpaired fish after the first pair is removed. The tank may be partitioned to house separate pairs but the partition should be opaque so the pairs do not visually impinge on each other's territory.

After pairing, the fish are prepared for spawning by maintaining an optimum environment in the aquarium, as per the previous chapters, and providing the best possible nutrition. The daily duration of light and tank temperature are also important. The pituitary gland, which sends hormones that activate the gonads, is stimulated to do so by constant summer day length and warm temperatures. The aquarium light should be set to provide 14 hours of light per day and the temperature should be a constant 80 °F. Also, provide rocks, flower pots, slate or other hard surfaces near the anemone to give the fish a spawn site. All that's needed from this point on is good aquarium management and patience. The fish will do what comes naturally when they mature.

The behavior of the pair usually gives an indication of impending spawning. The female is the dominant member of the pair since she is larger and seems to be chiefly responsible for defense of the territory. She is the one that attacks the fish, net,

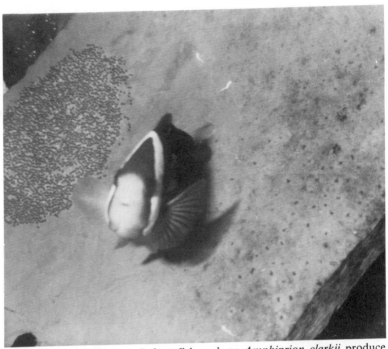

Figure 18. Large species of clownfish such as *Amphiprion clarkii* produce large nests. Some of these nests may have 1500 eggs. Although clownfish usually hide their nests if possible, they occasionally lay them out for all to see. The male guards proudly.

or hand that dares to invade their protectorate. The male, on the other hand, is the chief caretaker of the eggs and seems to be constantly appeasing the female to suffer his presence. Evidently there is a behavioral conflict in the female. She has on one side the stimulus to drive the male from the territory as she does with other members of her species and, conflictingly, she must keep him near her to be successful in reproduction. Obviously, there must be a frequent exchange of information between them to remind each other of their respective functions.

When the female attacks the male, he turns the attack away by head shaking and "chattering" directly in front of the female, a sort of submissive behavior. Just as the female must not actually attack the male, he must not actually flee her présence or reproduction will not succeed. As the attack is turned away, the male, and often the female also, engages in cleaning activity on any nearby hard surface. This is a displacement activity that turns

145

the fish away from attack and flee behavior and strengthens the pair bond. To the casual anthropomorphic eye the fish appear to be "playing tag" and "showing off", however, these are actually ritualized behavior patterns that strengthen the pair bond and prepare the fish for spawning. Unless you observe the fish carefully and critically each day, the first spawn will probably come as a surprise. As the time for spawning approaches, the fish may display heightened chasing activity and increased substrate biting. The female also becomes notably full in the abdomen. These conditions may persist for several days, especially with a first spawn, and you may think that the fish just don't know what to do. Take heart, though, for it will eventually occur. Common clownfish almost always spawn in late afternoon or early evening. The female's ovipositer extends early on the day of spawning and her fullness is quite pronounced. The pair select a spawn site an hour or two before the first eggs are laid and begin to clean the site by biting at the substrate while jerking the head from side to side. This activity becomes very intense as spawning approaches. At the end of the cleaning activity, the female begins to make passes over the cleaned area with her ovipositer lightly

Figure 19. A breeding pair of maroon clowns, *Premnas biaculeatus*. The large and agressive female of this species is not afraid to nip the hand of any unwary aquarist that ventures near the nest.

touching the hard surface. After several "dry" passes, the first bright orange eggs appear. They slip individually from the ovipositer, touch the substrate at one end and instantly adhere. A mass of very sticky, microscopic filaments attach the egg to the nest site. This is a flexible attachment and allows the eggs great side to side movement. The female leaves behind a single straight line of eggs across the nest site at each pass. Any eggs that do not adhere are quickly eaten by either parent. The female continues to lay a line of eggs at each pass until the patch of tightly packed eggs covers an area of one to four inches in diameter. The female pauses after every few passes and allows the male to fertilize the eggs she has just laid down. The male's motions are more rapid and fluttery than the female's and he seems to cover most of the enlarging patch of eggs each time he is active.

The male is the chief caretaker of the developing eggs. He frequently fans them with his pectoral and caudal fins, which aerates them and stimulates the developing embryo by movement. He also "mouths" the eggs, which consists of gentle biting at the egg patch. Although the parents are said to remove dead and diseased eggs this way, I have never seen them select and remove a dead egg. Eggs that die, quickly decompose and are swept off the nest by the general care patterns of the male. Any fallen eggs are usually consumed by one of the parents. The female also takes care of the nest in the same manner as the male, but her attentions are much less frequent.

Complete development to hatching takes place in 6 to 12 days depending primarily on temperature. The average time is 7 to 8 days at the typical temperature of 80 °F. Temperatures below 75 °F delay development and hatching. The bright orange of the new eggs becomes dark brown in about 3 days as the tissues of the developing embryo envelop the yolk. The dark pigment of the eyes becomes noticable at about day 4 and turn silvery at day 5 or 6 when the light reflecting pigment forms. On the day of hatching, the embryo develops a light violet sheen and the egg almost seems to bulge a little.

HATCHING

Normal hatching always occurs at night within two hours of first dark. Usually all the eggs in the nest hatch very quickly, within 15 or 20 minutes. If any eggs do not hatch at this time, chances are that they will wait for the following night to hatch.

Night hatching effectively reduces predation on the newly hatched larvae when they are near the bottom and are most vulnerable to bottom dwelling plankton predators, including their own parents. The adults will seek out and consume every larvae at first light if they remain together in the breeding tank.

The clownfish larvae is doubled up in the egg at hatching with the tail tucked in just below the head at the tip of the egg. For maximum reproductive economy, the eggs must be small and numerous; but for maximum survival, the larvae must be as large as possible at first feeding. Various species have different methods of resolving these conflicting demands. Most pelagic spawning species carry a large yolk sac in a small egg and hatch very early into an only partly developed pro-larval stage. The pro-larvae then continues development to a significantly larger first feeding larvae outside the physical constraints of a small egg. Pelagic eggs have no parental care, thus are subject to many predators and environmental hazards during their early development. Such species depend on production of vast numbers of eggs for survival. The egg of the mouth brooding jawfish is also

Figure 20. The clownfish egg just before hatching contains a miniature fish bent double inside the transparent membrane. The egg is only 2 mm long and the hatched larvae is 4 mm long. The eyes, fins and gut are fully developed at hatching and feeding begins within a few hours.

small, about a millimeter in diameter, but the larvae that hatches is comparatively large, about 4 millimeters long with a head that is almost one millimeter in diameter. This economy of space is achieved by wrapping the body of the larvae about the head during development. At hatching, after 5 to 7 days of incubation, the body unwinds from the head and, despite development in a small egg, the larvae is a respectable size and is ready to begin feeding almost immediately.

The clownfish egg is one of the largest of marine fish eggs at 1 mm in diameter and about 2 mm in length. Most larval fish hatch from the egg at the head by dissolving the egg shell with a protletic enzyme and then thrusting itself head first out of the egg case with tail and body movements. Clownfish are different, however, at hatching the egg case is ruptured at the tail just below the top of the egg. The tail and lower body then fall free and the larvae frees itself from the egg, which is still attached to the substrate, by a few rapid jerks of the tail and body. If the egg is not attached, the larvae is unable to easily free its head from the tip of the egg case and swims about pushing the egg case before it. This is usually fatal to the larvae for it can not respire normally, nor can it remove its egg case cap. Thus clownfish eggs should not be removed from the substrate before hatching.

LARVAL REARING

Clownfish spend the first two to three weeks of their life as pelagic larvae. In nature, this period is spent in the upper reaches of the sea feeding on the tiny animals that surround them in the plankton. Juvenile coloration develops as early as 8 days and as late as 20 days, and shortly after this metamorphosis they begin life on the bottom. The period of greatest concern to the marine fish breeder is the first two weeks, for this is the stage that is most difficult to maintain and feed.

Since the larvae are immediately pelagic at hatching, the first task is to set up a rearing tank that substitutes for the pelagic environment and to have it ready when the larvae hatch. This is relatively simple for a small scale operation. An adequate rearing environment can be prepared with a bare (no filter), high sided tank, one or two fine bubble air releasers and good lighting directly over the tank. With careful management up to about 100 fish can be taken through the larval stage (to about 3/8th inch long) in a 10 gallon tank, but greater success can be had more easily in tanks of 30 to 50 gallons.

The first major problem is recovering the larvae since they must be moved from the breeding tank to the rearing tank. There are three basic methods to achieve this transfer. First, and perhaps most feasible for the amateur marine breeder, is to remove as many of the newly hatched larvae from the breeding tank as possible. The larvae are strongly attracted to a light source after hatching, probably an adaptation to assure their movement into the upper water strata. It is an easy task to concentrate them with a flashlight in one corner of the aquarium because of this trait. Darkening the tank a few hours early on the day of hatch will bring them off earlier in the evening and hopefully prevent late night activity on the part of the aquarist. When the larvae have accumulated in one area of the tank they can be removed for transfer to the rearing tank by either siphoning them from the tank into a bucket or by capturing them with a cup or glass. The cup method is more time consuming and frustrating, but the chance of injury is less than that with the siphon. Of course, a net should never be used for the larvae can not withstand the physical abrasion.

The second method consists of removal and transfer of that part of the substrate containing the nest to the larval rearing tank and artificial hatching of the eggs. The eggs can be kept in good condition until hatching with an even curtain of bubbles gently rolling over the entire nest. Darkening the tank at the proper time causes the eggs to hatch. The third method requires a more elaborate set up with the breeding tank mounted directly over the larval tank and a constant water flow between the two tanks. This way the hatched larvae are automatically siphoned down to the rearing tanks and the two water masses, breeding and rearing, do not differ in quality. The intake from the rearing tank to the pumped return to the breeding tank must be well protected by a large surface area of fine mesh screen to prevent loss of larvae and the flow must be discontinued or greatly diminished to prevent loss of the larval fish food when the young fish begin to feed. Only those amateur breeders strongly inclined toward systems engineering will find it necessary to build such a unit.

Once the larvae have been transferred from the breeding tank to water of the same temperature and pH in the rearing tank, the real problems begin, and these are to provide the proper type and abundance of food organisms for the larval fish. There is a very good reason for the fantastic reproductive potential of most marine fish. This is that very, very few, one out of millions, survive the larval and juvenile stages in nature. Thus a great many potential lives must be launched to assure continuance of the species. These tiny larvae have little stored food and must begin feeding very soon after their systems are mature enough to capture food organisms. Even if the available food organisms are compatible with their nutritional and behavioral requirements, they must be abundant enough to provide energy for both movement and growth. Most attempts at rearing marine fish larvae fail for one or more of three reasons:

1. Improper physical and/or chemical environment.
2. Lack of an acceptable first food organism.
3. Lack of sufficient numbers of food organisms.

The proper physical and chemical rearing environment has already been discussed and it remains only to say that the tank bottom must be cleaned every day or two, and if possible, a partial water change effected with each cleaning. One water change of 50% to 80% once a week for the two to three week rearing period is all that is really necessary if a 10% to 20% change is not accomplished every two days. The more larvae that are reared in the tank, of course, the more important water changes become. Bottom cleaning is best done with a small siphon that picks up sediment without endangering larvae higher in the water column. Don't be alarmed if a green algal bloom develops in the rearing tank. This is actually good for the rearing environment as it provides nutrition for the food organisms present and takes up some of the metabolites produced by the animals in the tank. A white bloom, however, may be caused by bacteria and is usually detrimental to the larvae. Too many larvae, too many food organisms, lack of bottom cleaning, too much turbulence, and introduction of too much water from the food organism (rotifer) rearing tanks can all contribute to conditions that foster excessive bacterial growth. A thorough cleaning and water change with subsequent restocking of food organisms may save the larvae if a bacterial bloom is caught in the early stages. It is important to note that it is possible to rear limited numbers of clownfish in small tanks without any significant water changes over a three week period if care is taken to keep food organism populations at just the right levels.

Marine fish can be reared scientifically by precise measurement of water quality and food organism density, which is the best way to achieve reproducible results; or the aquarist can develop a "feel" for the requirements of the larvae and know from trial and error what will and what will not work. In actual practice, a blending of the two approaches seems to produce the best results. Perhaps the most important consideration, aside from the basics of tank, water, air and light, is to have the proper abundance of an acceptable food organism, usually rotifers or wild plankton. Three to eight food organisms per ml is a good level, although clownfish can survive on less especially if there are only a few larvae to feed. If you can't make an actual count of the number of food organisms by looking at a prepared sample in a counting chamber under a microscope, you'll have to use simpler techniques or even just go by visual estimate. With a little experience, it's possible to get to the point of looking into the tank and immediately knowing if the food levels are adequate. Five food organisms per ml translates to about 150 per ounce, so a shot glass of rearing tank water should contain over 150 food organisms. At this level there are 25 to 30 food organisms per teaspoon, an easy enough number to count. The best way to get an estimate of the actual level of food organisms in the tank is to count the number in four or five teaspoons and when the average count is between 25 and 30 there will be enough food organisms for good larval survival. Placing the sample in a shallow glass dish and examining it over a black background with a low power hand lens will facilitate the count. Maintaining the food organisms at this level will assure survival of most of the larvae.

Even though clownfish are about the largest and best developed of marine fish larvae when they begin feeding, new hatch brine shrimp are still too large for a first food. Of all the possible first foods that the aquarist can work with, there are four that give a good chance of success: wild plankton, cultured marine rotifers, fresh frozen rotifers and cultured marine ciliates. Other organisms and methods may also be successful, but these are ones that have actually worked. It may also be possible to rear a few clownfish with pulverized dry foods as a first offering and then a quick switch to new hatch brine shrimp as soon as the larvae are large enough to take them. This later method would require frequent tank cleanings and water changes and would be worth trying if the only other thing available was determination. A good quality dry flake food pulverized in a mortar and pestle, dry egg yolk and fresh water fish fry food are all possibles. If dry pulverized food is used, the water turbulence controlled by the air release should be kept as high as possible to keep the food in suspension as long as possible. It should not be so high, however, that the larvae can not control their own movements.

For those aquarists living near the coast, one of the easiest larval foods to obtain will be wild plankton. The relative ease or difficulty of collecting wild plankton every day for 10 to 15 days will determine for each individual case whether to culture a food organism or rely on plankton collection. The very smallest zooplankters are not needed by the relatively large clownfish larvae so it is possible to get by with a homemade plankton net and access to the tidal flow of ocean or bay. Wild plankton, although an excellent food for larval fish, has the drawbacks of great variability in quality and the possibility of introduction of planktonic predators and parasites. These problems, however, can be controlled by straining the plankton to eliminate organisms larger than 300 microns before feeding and through judicious use of light copper treatment.

A half meter plankton net of a 50 to 75 micron mesh can be purchased at most oceanic research supply houses and will do nicely to collect the necessary wild plankton. Professional plankton nets are expensive so a handy aquarist may wish to make one instead. Finding a material that will catch the smaller zooplankter and still pass enough water is the most difficult part of the project. A worn bed sheet may do the trick, but some experimentation is going to be required. Depending on the situation (quality of plankton, size of the rearing tank, and number of larvae), one collection of plankton per day may be adequate, but two may make for better success. Most wild plankton can survive for several hours in a bucket under light aeration so feeding can be spread out from one collection. The best chance of success will be had by combining wild plankton with cultured rotifers although either one alone is adequate. Observe the larval fish carefully to make sure that they are feeding. Actively feeding larvae frequently flex their body into an S shaped curve and then snap foreward suddenly to capture the prey immediately before them. The gut area will also become rounded with ingested food and take on a whitish color from plankton or rotifers. It is important to get them on new hatch brine shrimp as soon as possible for this will enhance their growth rate considerably. Add new hatch brine shrimp early in small quantities. Three to four days

153

Figure 21. A standard ½ meter plankton net with a quart collecting jar at the cod end. The rim is made of ¼ inch bar aluminum bent to the proper diameter and bolted together with stainless steel bolts. The net can be towed by a small boat or fished from a bridge in a tidal current.

after feeding is about right. The color of the gut will change from whitish to a pink or orange color when they begin to take the baby brine shrimp. They seem reluctant to take non-living foods until after they take on the adult coloration. At this point, somewhere between 10 and 20 days, they will take blended shrimp or scallop and pulverized dry flake food. Go easy on the dry flake food for it can cause the gut of young fish to bloat if overfed. Also keep the tank bottom clean once the switch to dry foods is begun. In fact, in a small rearing situation it is best to move the young fish to a tank with an undergravel filter as soon as all have taken on adult coloration and begin to stay near the tank side or bottom. Be careful not to overfeed baby brine shrimp at this point. The little fish seem not to have any mechanism that tells them to stop feeding when they have eaten enough and they can continue to feed on brine shrimp until they fall bloated to the bottom and die.

Marine fish culturists have looked long and hard for a good first food organism for marine fish larvae. Baby brine shrimp, although an excellent and readily available food, were of limited value because they are just too large for most marine fish larvae. What was needed was a small organism, about half the size or less of baby brine shrimp, that was easy to culture in large numbers, and that would be readily taken by the fish larvae and prove for their first nutritional needs. The National Marine Fisheries Service at the Fishery-Oceanography Center in La Jolla, California, was working with the culture of the northern anchovy and gulf croaker in 1969 and 70 and reported good success using cultures of the marine rotifer, *Brachionus plicatilis*. A starter culture of this organism was sent to our Florida pompano culture program in December, 1970, and proved to be a successful first food for pompano, spot fin pinfish, sea trout, redfish and other species. This organism is now widely used in fish culture throughout the

150 MICRONS

Figure 22. The marine rotifer, *Brachionus plicatilis,* adult and juvenile. This tiny marine animal is easy to culture and makes an excellent first food for many marine fish larvae. The adult female (left) carries 2 to 8 eggs on her tail when conditions for growth and reproduction are good. The eggs hatch into juvenile female rotifers (right) that become egg bearing adults in 24 hours. Such rapid reproduction allows phenomenal population growth and rotifer cultures must be carefully tended to keep population levels and culture conditions within proper bounds. Males appear in the population when temperature and/or food conditions are not favorable. Females and males produce a resting stage egg that survives even if the population dies. These eggs hatch when conditions improve and the rotifer population blooms again.

world and is available from many fish culture laboratories and several private companies. It was a short hop from food fish to tropical fish culture and *B. plicatilis* is probably used to some extent in all marine tropical fish culture operations.

B. plicatilis is not difficult to culture, but it does require daily care by the aquarist. The strongest and most nutritive rotifer cultures are those fed one celled marine algaes, however, cultures can be grown on dry activated yeast. There are many methodologies and techniques for culturing marine one celled algaes and rotifers and I can only present a few general principles and outline one simple culture method in this chapter. The best algaes to use are *Dunaliella, Isochrysis* and *Monochrysis* as these are easy for the rotifers to eat and provide good nutrition. The algae should be grown under conditions of constant illumination in one to five gallon containers and at temperatures of 75 to 80 °F. There should be no way that rotifers can get back to the algae cultures for these hungry little beasts will quickly wipe out the algae if they do. Feed the algae with a basic nutrient mix, sea water enriched with nitrate, phosphate and iron. One of the total

Figure 23. An inexpensive rotifer culture. A large population of rotifers can be grown and maintained for several weeks in a childs wading pool with a capacity of 100 to 300 gallons. Rotifers grown in the summer in such cultures can be frozen and stored for winter use.

element plant foods now on the market may do well for this purpose. Algae and rotifier culture requires use of considerable new salt water or great economy and reuse of a well filtered stock. Small cultures of algae and rotifers are dynamic; they reproduce and grow fiercely in the excellent conditions provided, and when the limits of growth are reached, they crash quickly into nothingness. Therefore each culture has to be harvested and renewed regularly to keep it in the constant growth phase. The growth of the rotifer cultures can be controlled somewhat by the amount of algae fed. Feeding can be increased several days before a hatch is due, thus stepping up production of rotifers for when they are most needed. The rotifer cultures are harvested by passing the culture through a fine screen, 25 to 50 microns, and collecting the concentrated rotifers for feeding to the rearing tank.

It is possible—not better, but possible—to rear rotifers for larval fish without the problems of algae culture. Dry activated yeast, the kind used in baking bread, can be fed in light suspension to rotifer cultures with good growth resulting. Yeast suspensions have been used for decades to feed small aquatic organisms.

Figure 24. Sorting sieves for rotifers and plankton sizing can be made from short pieces of four and six inch diameter PVC pipe. Industrial nylon and polyester fabrics in the range of 35 to 300 microns are attached to the pipe ends with PVC glue.

This is best done outside under sunlight since the yeast method encourages bacterial growth and sunlight helps control it. Rotifers can be grown in small volumes, 15 to 40 gallons, by the yeast method but do better in larger volumes of 90 to 200 gallons. A plastic kiddie pool about one foot deep and five feet across in partial shade with several air stones for turbulance makes a very good culture vessel. The yeast for feeding to the rotifers is prepared by dissolving about a tablespoon of the dry yeast in a pint of warm water. The resulting milky suspension can be kept in the refrigerator for several days and fed to the cultures as required. The rotifer cultures should be fed the yeast solution once a day for maintenance and low harvest rate and twice a day for maximum harvest. The bottom of small volume cultures should be siphoned every few days and any water loss made up with clean water. The proper amount of the yeast suspension to feed is that amount that keeps the culture water slightly milky for several hours after feeding. It is wise to have several such cultures, for yeast fed rotifer cultures are a bit more precarious then algae fed cultures. Without culturing, there is no way to develop the numbers of rotifers necessary for even a small clownfish rearing experiment. Low temperatures, below 70°F, depress rotifer reproduction so accomodation must be made for winter conditions.

It is also possible to rear clownfish larvae solely on frozen rotifers as a first food. The rotifers are taken from dense cultures, strained and washed, and then frozen in salt water in small blocks. The frozen blocks are thawed just before feeding in a cup or two of salt water and then fed to the rearing tank. The rotifers are dead, of course, but if tank turbulence is adequate, they do not immediately settle out. They remain in the water column long enough for the clownfish larvae to obtain adequate food. They do settle fairly quickly, however, and the bottom must be siphoned daily if frozen rotifers are used. Also, more than one feeding per day is necessary since the rotifers are not continuously available to the larval fish. Two and perhaps three feedings are necessary each day depending on tank conditions. This technique makes it possible to rear large amounts of rotifers in summer, when culture conditions are good outdoors, and then save them for winter rearing runs. New hatched brine shrimp must be provided as soon as possible for best success when frozen rotifers are used as a first larval food.

Marine ciliates in the genus *Euplotes* have been used successfully to rear limited numbers of clownfish larvae at the Wilhelma Aquarium in Germany. However, the most successful trials with *Euplotes* also included a low density of various other zooplankters produced by a tank rich with invertebrate populations. *Euplotes* are smaller and apparently less nutritious for larval fish than rotifers, but they can bridge the gap from first feeding to baby brine shrimp for some larvae. Living *Euplotes* cultures can be obtained from some scientific supply houses and can be cultured with yeast suspensions as described for rotifers. Potato water, algal cultures and decomposing meat can also create rich cultures of *Euplotes*.

JUVENILE GROWTH

When the young clownfish are fully colored and about ¼ to ½ inch long they should be moved to a tank with an established filter. They will grow faster and stronger in bottom environment after this stage of development is attained. Gradually wean them from dependence on baby brine shrimp to standard marine tropical fish foods.

OTHER SPECIES

The amateur marine fish breeder must concentrate on those species that will reproduce readily in the aquaria and that have hardy eggs and/or early larvae that allow recovery. The neon goby and the royal gramma are two species that fill these requirements. Both species can be paired by the same basic method as described for clownfish, for a mated pair will not tolerate other individuals in their tank space. Despite this similarity, there are many biological differences between them. The male is usually the larger of the pair in both neon gobies and royal grammas and the abdominal fullness of the active female is the prominent sexual difference.

Neon gobies attach their eggs to the substrate very much like clownfish, but their nests are more secretive. They place their eggs under shells and rocks and the presence of the nest is seldom known until the tank is suddenly filled with tiny, transparent hatchlings. Hatching usually takes place at night, but it is not uncommon for a nest to hatch in the daytime. The male is in charge of the nest and spends much time working over the eggs. The presence of a nest can be suspected if the male is observed entering and leaving the same small opening with great frequency.

Royal grammas have only recently been spawned and reared successfully. Their reproductive mode has been little known up to this point. Because their relatives, the sea basses, produce planktonic eggs, it was thought that the grammas may also release free floating eggs. Tank spawns, however, have demonstrated that royal grammas are secretive nest builders. The male selects a nest site hidden deep in some crevice or under a rock. He actively cleans this hidden area of stones and shells until the nest site meets his specifications. He then brings algal strands into the nest area until it appears filled with only a small entry hòle visible. The female is enticed into the nest at about this point, the male also enters and up to 30 minutes may pass before either of them leave the nest. During this period, the female lays from 20 to 100 large eggs that have numerous long, sticky filaments extending from their surface that serve to bind the eggs to each other and to the surrounding algal mass.

Figure 25. Royal gramma, *Gramma loreto,* are secretive spawners. These eggs were laid in a nest of *Entromorpha* algae carefully built by the male several days before the spawn. the eggs have small "pimples" on their surface, each with several long sticky threads that bind the eggs to each other and the strands of algae. Each egg contains several oil droplets, perhaps left over from an ancient time when the eggs were pelagic.

The eggs are relatively large, about one millimeter in diameter, and have six or more small oil droplets. They are not transparent, but have a yellowish, translucent appearance. The female may enter the nest every day or two for a month or more and repeat the performance each time. The male cares for the eggs in the nest periodically, but the eggs do not seem to require the nearly constant care a male clownfish gives to his nest. The eggs develop very slowly, 5 to 7 days from fertilization to hatching, and hatch in the daily sequence that they were laid. Thus, only a few are ready to hatch each night. The constant daily hatch of larvae may be an adaptation to constantly release larvae throughout the spawning season to take advantage of conditions favorable for survival whenever they may occur. The larvae are relatively large and hardy, but recovery is complicated by the hatch and release of only a few per night. They somehow find their way out of the nest site and into the upper water column after hatching. Hatching always takes place within a few hours after dark, similar to clownfish hatching. The male is in the nest at hatching, but does not seem to aid the hatchlings in their journey to the plankton rich, upper water levels. The small transparent larvae are ready to feed on the day after hatching and grow very fast under the right conditions.

Although not totally comprehensive, this chapter on marine fish breeding is a new addition to books on marine aquariums. It is a sign of the changes developing in the hobby and an indication of new directions. We know relatively little of the biology of many of the creatures that find their way into our marine aquariums. Reports of observations and breeding attempts by amateur marine aqauarists, even those published in local society newsletters, add much to our knowledge, understanding, and enjoyment of the ocean life within our homes. So be encouraged to observe, think, and share your findings with fellow marine aquarists.

SELECTED REFERENCES

This is by no means a complete listing for there are many books available that deal with tropical marine fishes and invertebrates, marine aquariums, and things of the sea. The books listed below, however, have been of value and interest to me and they should also benefit other marine aquarists.

Allen, Gerald R. 1980
  Butterfly and Angelfishes of the World. Vol. 2: Atlantic Ocean, Caribbean Sea, Red Sea, Indo-Pacific. Wiley-Interscience, New York, N.Y. 352 pp.
Allen, Gerald R. 1980
  Anemonefishes of the World: Species, Care, and Breeding. Aquarium Systems, Mentor, Ohio 104 pp.
Allen, Gerald R. 1975
  The Anemonefishes: Their Classification and Biology. (2nd Edition) T.F.H. Publications, Inc., Neptune, N.J. 352 pp.
Atz, James W. and Douglas Faulkner 1971
  Aquarium Fishes: Their Beauty, History and Care. The Viking Press. New York, N.Y. 112 pp.
Bellomy, Mildred D. 1969
  Encyclopedia of Sea Horses. T.F.H. Publications, Inc. Neptune, N.J.
Bohlke, James E. and Charles C. Chaplin 1968
  Fishes of the Bahamas and Adjacent Tropical Waters. Livingston Publishing Co. Wynnewood, Pa. 771 pp.
Breder, Charles M. Jr. and Donn E. Rosen 1966
  Modes of Reproduction in Fishes. T.F.H. Publications, Inc. Neptune, N.J.
Chaplin, Charles C.G. 1972
  Fishwatchers Guide to West Atlantic Coral Reefs. Livingston Publishing Co., Wynnewood, Pa.
Colin, Patrick 1975
  The Neon Gobies. T.F.H. Publications, Inc. Neptune, N.J. 304 pp.
de Graaf, Frank 1973
  Marine Aquarium Guide. The Pet Library, Ltd. London, England, 284 pp.
Herald, E.S. 1961
  Living Fishes of the World. Doubleday and Co., Garden City, N.Y. 304 pp.
Hess, Deb and John Stevely 1981
  The Biology of Marine Aquarium Fishes Collected in Monroe County, Florida. NOAA Technical Memorandum, NMFS-SEFC - 59. pp 26-83.
Keenleyside, Miles H.A. 1979
  Diversity and Adaptation in Fish Behavior. Springer-Verlag, New York, N.Y. 208 pp.
Kingsford, Edward 1979
  Marine Aquarium Compatibility Guide. Palmetto Publishing Company, St. Petersburg, Fla. 70 pp.
Kingsford, Edward 1975
  Treatment of Exotic Marine Fish Diseases. Palmetto Publishing Co., St. Petersburg, Fla. 92 pp.

Klocek, Rodger and John Kolman 1976
   Marines (The Fishes). Marine Hobbyist News Publications, Bloomington, Ill. 144 pp.
Needham, James G., F.E. Lutz, P.S. Welch and P.S. Galtsoff, Ed. 1937
   Culture Methods for Invertebrate Animals. Comstock Publishing Company. Dover Edition 1959. Dover Publications, New York, N.Y. 590 pp.
Palko, Barbara J. 1981
   A Balanced Marine Aquarium. NOAA Technical Memorandum, NMFS-SEFC - 59. pp 1-25.
Quick, Joe A. Jr. 1977
   Marine Disease Primer: Book One, A guide to disease prevention in aquarium fishes and invertebrates. Marine Hobbyist News Publications. Bloomington, Ill. 47 pp.
Randall, John E. 1965
   Food Habits of Reef Fishes of the West Indies. In Studies in Tropical Oceanography, Vol. 5. pp 665-840.
Randall, John E. 1968
   Caribbean Reef Fishes. T.F.H. Publications, Neptune, N.J. 318 pp.
Spotte, Stephen H. 1973
   Marine Aquarium Keeping: The Science, Animals and Art. Wiley-Interscience, New York, N.Y. 171 pp.
Spotte, Stephen H. 1970
   Fish and Invertebrate Culture: Water Management in Closed Systems. Wiley-Interscience. New York, N.Y. 145 pp.
Steene, Rodger C. 1979
   Butterfly and Angelfishes of the World. Vol. 1: Australia. Wiley-Interscience. New York, N.Y. 144 pp.
Straughan, Robert P.L. 1970
   The Salt Water Aquarium in the Home. A.S. Barnes and Company. Cranbury, N.J. 360 pp.
Thresher, Ronald E. 1980
   Reef Fish: Behavior and Ecology on the Reef and in the Aquarium. Palmetto Publishing Company, St. Petersburg, Fla. 171 pp.
Walls, Jerry G. 1975
   Fishes of the Northern Gulf of Mexico. T.F.H. Publications, Inc. Neptune, N.J.

Periodicals
Freshwater and Marine Aquarium Magazine. Don Dewey, Ed., Sierra Madre, Calif.
Tropical Fish Hobbyist. Marshall E. Ostrow, Ed., Neptune, N.J.

WEIGHTS, MEASURES AND
USEFUL DATA

ABBREVIATIONS

Selected Chemical Elements

Barium	Ba	Hydrogen	H	Phosphorous	P
Boron	B	Iodine	I	Potassium	K
Bromine	Br	Iron	Fe	Silicon	Si
Calcium	Ca	Lead	Pb	Silver	Ag
Carbon	C	Magnesium	Mg	Sodium	Na
Chlorine	Cl	Manganese	Mn	Strontium	Sr
Cobalt	Co	Mercury	Hg	Sulfur	S
Copper	Cu	Nitrogen	N	Tin	Sn
Flourine	F	Oxygen	O	Zinc	Zn

pH - Hydrogen ion concentration (power of hydrogen)
ppt or o/oo - parts per thousand
ppm - parts per million
SG - specific gravity
°F - degrees in Fahrenheit
°C - degrees in Centigrade

TEMPERATURE

Centigrade	0	100	18.3	20	21.1	23.9	25	30	32.2	35
Fahrenheit	32	212	65	68	70	75	77	86	90	95

To convert °F to °C.

$$\frac{(°F - 32)}{1.8} = °C$$

To convert °C to °F.

$$(°C \times 1.8) + 32 = °F$$

LIQUID MEASURE

one cc (cubic centimeter) = 1 ml, approximately 1/20 drop
one ml (milliliter) = 1 cc, 1/1000 liter
one L (liter) = 1000 ml, 1.06 qt, 2.1 pt
20 large drops or 25 small drops = approximately 1 ml
one tsp (teaspoon) = 5 ml, 1/6 fl oz
one tbsp (tablespoon) = 3 tsp, ½ fl oz, 15 ml
one fl oz (fluid ounce) = 2 tbsp, 6 tsp, 29.6 ml
one cup = 8 fl oz, 236.8 ml
one pt (pint) = 16 fl oz, 473.2 ml
one qt (quart) = 32 fl oz, 2 pt, 946.3 ml, .95 L
one gal (gallon) = 128 fl oz, 8 pt, 4 qt, 3.8 L, 231 cubic inches

WEIGHT

one mg (milligram) = 1/1000 g
one g (gram) = 1000 mg, 15.4 gr, .035 oz
one k (killogram) = 1000 g, 35 oz, 2.2 lbs
one gr (grain) = .65 g
one oz (ounce) = 28.35 g
one lb (pound) = 16 oz, 454 g, .45 k

LENGTH

one μ (micron) = 1/1000 mm
one mm (millimeter) = 1/10 cm, 1000 μ
one cm (centimeter) = 10 mm, .39 in
one m (meter) = 1000 mm, 100 cm, 39.37 in, 3.28 ft
one in (inch) = 25.4 mm, 2.54 cm
one ft (foot) = 12 in, 30.48 cm, .3 m
one yd (yard) = 3 ft, 91.44 cm, .91 m

WATER DATA

one cu ft (cubic foot) of sea water = 64 lbs, 29.02k, 7.5 gal, 28.4 L
1728 cu in (cubic inches), 3785.4 cc

one gallon of sea water = 8.5 lbs, 3.86 k, 231 cu in

To find the number of gallons in a rectangular or square tank —

Multiply the length × width × height in inches and divide by 231.

To find the number of gallons in a cylindrical tank —

Multiply the diameter squared × .8 × the height in inches and divide by 231.

Full strength sea water contains 30 to 37 parts per thousand (30 to 37 grams per killogram) of salts. True specific gravity of this range is 1.0222 to 1.0275.

At 77 °F (25 °C) the specific gravity of 30 to 37 ppt sea water ranges from 1.0196 to 1.0249.

INDEX